Electric Pressure Cooker Cookbook

100 Quick, Easy, and Healthy Recipes for Electric Pressure Cookers

Table of Contents

Chicken Corn Chowder with Pumpkin
Zuppa Toscana
Simple 'n Quick Miso Soup
Moroccan Red Lentil Soup
Butternut Squash Bisque
Julia Child's French Onion Soup (Electric Pressure Cooker Version)

Meat Entrees

Pork

Apples & Onions Pork Tenderloin
Pork Chops & Cabbage
Simple Braised Pork
Pressure-Cooker Pork Vindaloo
Pork Chops w/ Creamy Mushroom Gravy
Shredded BBQ Pork
Pork Sirloin Tip Roast
Braised Pork w/ Peas and White Beans
Pressure-Cooker Herbed Pork Roast
Kalua Pig in a Pressure Cooker

Chicken

Balsamic Chicken Breasts and Pearl Onions
Hawaiian BBQ Chicken
Curried Chicken and Spinach
Chicken Prosciutto Rolls
Pressure-Cooker Chicken Gumbo
Whole Chicken in a Pressure Cooker
Pesto Chicken w/ Carrots + New Potatoes
Teriyaki Chicken Bowls
Coconut Chicken Curry
Lemon-Olive Ligurian Chicken
Easy Buffalo Chicken Wings
Spicy Cornish Game Hen
Cranberry Turkey Wings
Braised Quill w/ a Carrot + Fennel Nest

Introduction

If you haven't been incorporating an electric pressure cooker into your cooking routine, you are really missing out! Electric pressure cookers come with the convenience of slow cookers and the kind of speed rivaled only by programmable microwaves. However, cooking with an electric pressure cooker is way healthier than relying on a microwave. In fact, pressure cooking is the healthiest cooking method there is.

Why, you ask? For starters, the nutrients in food are slowly reduced as the food is cooked, so the faster the cooking method, the fewer nutrients escape. So, because you can cook foods like beans and rice between 1-5 minutes, they retain nearly all of their nutritional value. This means veggies, meat, grains, and any other kind of food you can think of will be at its healthiest and most easily-digested.

You can cook all your meals in an electric pressure cooker, even breakfasts and desserts. If you have been wanting to eat healthier, but are finding that a lot of recipes and cooking methods don't fit well into your busy lifestyle, an electric pressure cooker is the way to go. You can also start buying cheaper cuts of meat and dried beans (which are more affordable in bulk than canned beans), because pressure cookers transform those tough cuts and tough foods into mouthwatering dishes. Eating healthy doesn't have to be expensive or difficult!

The first few chapters of this book serve as your guide to everything about electric pressure cookers. You'll learn a bit about their history, why they're better than stove top pressure cookers, and how they work. You'll also learn some useful tips about how to clean your pressure cooker, what brands are the most popular (and why), and how to convert your favorite slow cooker recipes to the faster, more efficient pressure cooker. After that, you'll find 100 recipes specifically designed for the electric pressure cooker, from breakfast to lunch to dinner, to vegan to meat lover's. You don't want to delay electric pressure cooking any longer!

Chapter 1 - What Were The First Pressure Cookers Like?

The first pressure cookers looked very little like the kitchen tool we know and love today. They were ugly, unwieldy things that looked like they would be more at home in an industrial factory than a kitchen. The first pressure cooker even had an ugly name - the "digester." Denis Papin, the pressure cooker's inventor, came up with that name. His intention was that his creation would be able to "digest" bones and extract the vitamins within. This was accomplished by heating water to extremely high temperatures in an airtight container, so the steam couldn't escape. This led to high amounts of pressure build-up, raising water's boiling point. After accidents where the digester exploded, Papin figured out the steam had to be released eventually, so he added a steam release valve.

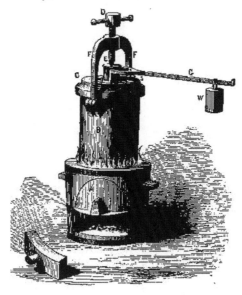

Papin was especially interested in how the digester could benefit the poor, who had limited access to food and needed to make the most of everything they had, but the tool proved to be too expensive for anyone but the elite. The first people who sampled food from the digester were the rich and famous - the king of France was there, and gave the invention rave reviews.

A 1970's pressure cooker

That was in the 17th century, and by the 19th century, the digester was being used primarily by the military who needed fast meals, or canners who wanted to preserve large quantities of meat to sell. Time went on, and finally, pressure cooking became more mainstream. In 1915, the Journal of Home Economics rechristened the digester, "the pressure cooker," and by the 1930's, the cooker's crude design had slimmed down. This was also around the time home canning became especially popular. WWII erupted, and people were encouraged to preserve fresh foods and waste nothing. While production of new pressure cookers was halted in favor of war supplies, new designs started to pop up outside of the US, and by the end of the war, people started buying new pressure cookers again. In the 1970's, companies published cookbooks and got creative about how people could use pressure cookers. The health food movement was especially fond of the pressure cooker, as the cooker's speed preserved more vegetable nutrients than other cooking methods.

The very first electric pressure cooker didn't appear until 1991. Until that time, everyone used stove top pressure cookers, and while they offered a lot of power, they were not convenient for those who couldn't stand by the stove and adjust the burner in order to maintain pressure. With the new electric models came features like a timer and an electric heat source that automatically maintained the temperature. No one is quite sure how the first electric pressure cooker came to be, but a Chinese scientist - Yong-Guang Wang - holds the very first patent.

There have been three generations of electric pressure cookers. The first just came with a timer, and was otherwise very similar to the stove top models. The second generation was capable of delaying cooking and came with a countdown timer, so once the selected pressure was reached, you could see how much longer a recipe would take. The third generation - the most modern - comes with advanced pre-sets that are totally programmable, so you have absolute control over temperature, time, and pressure. Though its exact origins may be a bit murky, the benefits of electric pressure cookers are anything but!

Chapter 2 - What Are The Advantages Of An Electric Pressure Cooker?

Before the invention of the pressure cooker, water always had the same boiling point. Once it reaches 212-degrees Fahrenheit, that's as hot as it could go. However, your altitude affects boiling point. A higher elevation means less pressure and therefore, a lower boiling point. For example, on top of Mount Everest, water boils at 62-degrees. At first thought, it might seem that cooking food would take *less* time when you're up really high - the water boils at only 62-degrees and it doesn't take long to get there! However, even though the water is boiling, it's still only 62-degrees, and food like chicken needs to be at least 165-degrees to be safe to eat. Getting to that temperature would take forever when your water can only get as hot as 62-degrees.

This is where an invention like the pressure cooker comes in handy, because it can get water above its boiling point very quickly through the buildup of pressure. All pressure cookers have this basic function and benefits over other cooking methods (boiling, grilling, baking), but electric pressure cookers in particular come with additional advantages:

- They monitor the pressure for you

  With a stove top pressure cooker, the heat source comes from a burner. You have to lower or increase the flame in order to maintain the appropriate pressure for your recipe. Electric pressure cookers do all that for you, so the pressure always remains consistent. You can leave the pressure cooker like you would a slow cooker, and do other chores or just relax while your dinner cooks.

- You don't have to guess about timing

  One of the first features on the electric pressure cooker was a timer. Instead of keeping track of time all by yourself, you just set the timer and when it goes off, you're ready to go. Since it takes time to reach pressure, stove top pressure cookers are all different, while with electric pressure cookers, it always takes about 25 minutes to reach full pressure, and then however long the recipe called for. All that is factored into the timer, so you don't have to wait to start counting and risk messing up.

- They are safer

  Pressure cookers have a reputation of being a little distance. While explosions are pretty much a non-issue, stove top pressure cookers still come with some risk. Electric ones, on the other hand, are usually loaded with safety features designed to deal with the high amounts of pressure, hot temperatures, and so on. You can rest easy with an electric pressure cooker on your counter.

- They're more energy-efficient

  Even with their airtight construction, stove top pressure cookers lose heat. Electric pressure cookers, however, behave like thermoses and keep the heat packed inside. Upon closer examination, it has been discovered that an electric pressure cooker can be up to 60% more efficient than a stove top pressure cooker on an (electric) stove. Not one drop of electricity is wasted!

- They're easier to clean

  Cleaning your pressure cooker well is very important, since food bits and odors tend to stick around. Electric pressure cookers have been made so they clean up easily - they often have an inner pot that you remove and submerge in water. I'll get into more details later when it comes to a
  cleaning routine.

Electric pressure cookers do have some disadvantages, and it's important to be knowledgeable about all the differences. The biggest drawback when comparing stove top vs. electric has to do with power. Stove top pressure cookers can usually reach a max PSI (pounds per square inch) of 15, while electric pressure cookers peak at around 10 or 12. This means food cooks faster on a stove top. However, the time difference is relatively small, and when you factor in the convenience of leaving an electric pressure cooker and doing other things while it cooks, those few PSIs aren't really a good enough reason to forgo electric. I'll tell you more about PSI in the next chapter.

So, how do you know if an electric pressure cooker is right for you? If you meet most or all of the following criteria, you should definitely buy an electric pressure cooker:

- You want to reduce the time you spend cooking
- You want to make healthier food
- You don't want to have to stand over a stove
- You're a busy person who often has to order out for dinner
- You have kids and pets who often mess around in the kitchen

- You have a stove top pressure cooker, and want something more convenient

Chapter 3 - How Does An Electric Pressure Cooker Work?

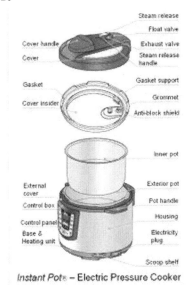

Instant Pot – Electric Pressure Cooker

Before you start using an electric pressure cooker, you should know the basic structure and what all the parts do. There are three essential pieces: the inner pot, the locking lid, and base. The inner pot is where all the food rests, and in recent years, they have become removable for easier cleaning. They are usually constructed from aluminum or stainless steel, which is technically dishwasher-safe, but will start to wear down after too many cycles. Most inner pots are between 3-6 quarts, which is perfect for most families.

The lid lock is what seals the pressure inside the pressure cooker. It has a gasket or sealing ring which clamps the lid shut to the pressure cooker body. The lid must be in the locked position. Many electric cookers have a pin lock (sometimes called a float valve), which is pushed into place by high amounts of pressure, preventing the lid from accidentally popping open and releasing tons of dangerous, hot steam. Once it pops into place, you know that top pressure has been released. There are often additional safety valves that prevent accidental pressure release, like anti-block shields.

The last main part of an electric pressure cooker is the base, which contains the heating unit and control box. The heating unit is obviously electricity-based, and the control box is essentially the "brain" of your pressure cooker. This box is responsible for monitoring the cooker's pressure and temperature. Nearly all modern electric pressure cookers are equipped with sensors that will sound an alarm if the pressure cooker is unsafe to use. It will also cut off the heating element, preventing you from turning it on until the problem is solved. You control the box with the control panel, which is similar to modern microwaves. This control panel has all sorts of useful cooking pre-sets, like "Sauté" or "Warm," as well as controls for specific foods and dishes like beans, rice, soup, and so on.

On some electric pressure cookers, like Presto brand ones, you attach a knob-like piece on top of the pressure cooker lid. This is called the pressure regulator, and it controls the amount of pressure. The regulator on pressure cookers physically rocks when it starts going up in pressure. These are also usually the models of electric pressure cooker where you select a temperature on a dial. If the regulator starts shaking longer than 2 minutes, turn down the heat until it only rocks occasionally. This lets you know the electric pressure cooker is maintaining pressure. These are always present on stove top pressure cookers, though some models (the Presto Electric Pressure Cooker) still have one.

Important safety tip
Never try to open the pressure cooker as it is cooking. It will be like opening a bottle of soda after it's been violently shaken. If you need to open it, you have to turn off the cooker and reduce the pressure all the way.

As you become more familiar with the pressure cooker, you will notice that many recipes talk about putting food in a steamer basket or on top of a trivet. These are necessary for cooking food that cannot touch the bottom of the pressure cooker, like whole eggs (for hard-boiled eggs). You basically just put food in the steamer basket and lower it into the pressure cooker, which will always have some sort of liquid in it to generate steam. The pressure cooker "steams" the food in the basket. The trivet is often used for making cakes and other similar foods. You pour all the ingredients into a bowl, wrap the bowl in foil, and then place it on top of the trivet. The electric pressure cooker then acts like an oven and bakes the food.

The next important thing to know about electric pressure cookers is how to actually program one. PSI, which as I mentioned earlier stands for "pounds per square inch," is the term used to describe the amount of pressure in the pressure cooker. As pressure rises, so does the temperature. This chart is from the website *hip pressure cooking* and shows how the two are connected.

bar	PSI	°F	°C
1.03	15	250	121
1	14.5	249	120.6
.9	13.1	246	119
.8	11.6	243	117
.7	10.2	239	116
.6	8.7	237	114
.5	7.3	233	112
.4	5.8	229	110
.3	4.4	225	107
.2	2.9	221	105
.1	1.5	217	103

If you are curious about what pressure your electric pressure cooker can reach, there are three different PSIs to look for: operating pressure, valve release pressure, and warping pressure. The operating pressure is the PSI the cooker actually cooks, or the one that you set for your recipe. The valve release pressure is the PSI the cooker reaches when it needs to start releasing pressure, in order to prevent explosion. This is usually a few PSI more than the operating pressure, and is necessary to maintain the pressure you want for your recipe. You can usually find this information on the bottom of the electric cooker's pressure release valve. The warping pressure is the PSI that will cause damage to the pressure cooker. You never want your cooker to reach this.

Electric pressure cookers often don't have settings for specific PSI. Instead, you can choose to set your pressure cooker to "low" or "high." A low setting usually means the PSI range will be between 6-8, while high puts the cooker between 9-12, depending on how much PSI your specific electric cooker can have. There currently aren't any electric pressure cookers that can maintain 15 psi (250-degrees F) - they usually get to about 10-12 PSI.

Once the timer for your recipe goes off, it's time to release the pressure. This part is very important, since it can actually affect how the recipe turns out. You have two options, and should always go with the option the recipe calls for.

Important safety tip
Always turn away from the pressure cooker as the pressure is released, or you will get a faceful of skin-searing steam!

"Quick-release" is when you turn the steam release handle to the "venting" position. The steam comes out faster through this quick-release method and de-pressurizes the cooker in 60-90 seconds. The other way is the natural-release method, which is when you leave the cooker alone and the steam slowly releases through various holes in the lid that have been designed for this purpose. Just turn off the cooker and wait 8-25 minutes. Once the float valve/pin lock has gone all the way down, the pressure is all gone.

And that's it! There are some other useful tips and terms that will come in hand, but I'll sprinkle those in through the different recipes as they come up. Next up, the best ways to clean your pressure cooker.

Chapter 4- How Do I Keep My Electric Pressure Cooker Clean?

A dirty pressure cooker is gross. It will harbor the smells of every meal you've ever cooked in it, and will taint every future meal. You won't ever want to use it, and you'll be missing out on the best way to prepare just about any type of food. There are several parts to clean, but if you develop a habit of it, cleaning an electric pressure cooker can be easy.

Must-know cleaning tip
Do NOT use a scratchy sponge to clean the gasket. The abrasive surface wears down the silicone.

The first part you need to clean is the lid. Even if you decide to leave the inner pot soaking for a while and leave the real clean-up for later, you don't want to save the lid. Most of the gross oils and smells catch on the lid. The gasket should be removed after every use and cleaned. Never use a dishwasher to clean the gasket, since they are made from silicon (few are made from rubber), and will warp and break in a dishwasher. Soak the gasket for about 15 minutes in mild dish soap and hot water. If stains persist, you can use an all-purpose cleaner made for cleaning oil from grills, and then soak again for a few minutes before rinsing well. If your gasket has an especially nasty odor, you can try soaking it in vinegar and baking soda, but sometimes you just have to replace that piece of the pressure cooker. Just the gasket part is pretty inexpensive.

Must-know cleaning tip
Your gasket might need to be oiled before use. Read your pressure cooker manual.

The next piece you should clean on the lid is the exhaust valve. You don't have to clean it after *every* use, but you should clean it after you cook rice or pasta. The starch in these foods clogs up the valve, which makes quick-release difficult. Take off the valve cover to clean, and remove the valve. Use something thin and metallic (like a needle) to scrap out any gunk. Don't use a toothpick, because they can easily break and be stuck forever in the valve.

Most electric pressure cookers come with a removable inner pot. You can either wash by hand using a non-scratchy sponge, soap, and hot water, or run it through the dishwasher. If your pressure cooker has a condensation cup, you'll want to clean and dry that well, too.

For the outside of the cooker, just wipe it down when it gets stained. You can use any product you would use on stainless steel and a paper towel. If you store your pressure cooker underneath your counters, do not leave the lid on. This traps any remaining smells, leaving them to ruminate inside your pressure cooker again. Instead, let the cooker air out. If there's a bit of dust inside when you take it out again, just give it a brief rinse.

Chapter 5 - Which Electric Pressure Cooker Should I Choose?

There are a lot of electric pressure cookers out there, so it can be hard to decide which one to get. There are five things to consider when you're shopping: capacity, functions, construction, replacement parts, and price. The capacity basically just means how big you want your pressure cooker to be. The most common models are 6 and 8 quarts, which are usually enough to make meals for families and groups. It's also easy to split a recipe into two batches, especially with fast-cooking dishes like vegetables, so even if you are cooking a meal for a crowd, a 6-quart model is acceptable.

> **Buying Tip**
> Pressure cookers should only be filled ⅔ of the way. Keep that in mind when you're looking at capacity.

The next thing to consider is functionality. Do you want an electric pressure cooker with a lot of pre-sets (Sauté, Warm, Beans, Rice, etc.) so you don't have to determine pressure and time? Or do you want something more basic with just a low and high setting? If you've never used an electric pressure cooker before, you might want to get one where you just hit one button, so you can make lots of basic dishes like soup until you figure out how to program more manual options.

Construction is very important when shopping for an electric pressure cooker. If the cooker is made from inferior materials, it won't last very long. Think about how often you plan on using the cooker. If you want to use it a lot, you'll want to go with stainless steel, since it isn't as prone to staining and odor retention.

You should also do some research on how expensive replacement parts are for a particular pressure cooker. I mentioned earlier that replacement gaskets are usually affordable, but many brands charge quite a bit for a basic part. Before you buy, look into the cost of replacing parts like the gasket, inner pot, and so on.

The last (but certainly not least) factor is the sticker price. The average price for a pressure cooker is between $200-$300, while the more expensive ones can get closer to $500. Capacity and features have a lot to do with the price, so if you want a big pressure cooker with lots of settings and the newest technology, you'll be spending a pretty penny. Before you go to a store or look online, make a list of everything you want in an electric pressure cooker, using the first four tips as a guide. You'll be able to see how much your dream pressure cooker costs, and if it's too expensive, start prioritizing. Do you really *need* the 8-quart model, or are you okay with making multiple batches if necessary? While 14 smart programs are nice, are 10 just as good if you save a hundred dollars?

There are lots of brands out there, and some are better than others. Here are five of the most popular brands and the kinds of features their models offer:

- Instant Pot

The Instant Pot, the IP-LUX60 specifically, has a 6-in-1 function, so the pressure cooker acts like a slow cooker, rice cooker, steamer, warmer, and sauté/browner in addition to its pressure cooker capabilities. It has 10 pre-set programs, three modes, and three temperatures in its sauté/browning and slow cooking mode. Some other cool features include a 24-hour delay cooking timer and durable stainless steel body and steamer.

- Cuisinart

The 6-quart Cuisinart electric pressure cooker boasts pre-sets, a 99-minute timer for longer recipes, 6 pressure settings, and a dishwasher-safe pot and trivet. Cuisinart is known for its quality products, so it makes sense that their electric pressure cooker is so popular. The pot and trivet are also non-stick, which might be a problem, since non-stick surfaces tend to chip after time and hold smells.

- Fagor

The 6-quart pressure cooker is also a rice cooker and slow cooker, with a brushed stainless-steel body and functions like Keep Warm and Automatic Rice Cooking. You can delay cooking for up to 8 hours, and the removable parts of the cooker (besides the gasket, obviously) are dishwasher-safe.

- Secura

The Secura 6-in-1 electric pressure cooker comes at a pretty good deal for a cooker with a stainless-steel pot. You can find it for just over $100, and it has browning, steaming, and sauté functions, and can be used as a slow cooker, rice cooker, or pressure cooker. The one downside is it doesn't have a manual option.

- Nesco

Nesco makes small kitchen appliances, and their PC6-25P electric pressure cooker is a great size (6 quarts) for most kitchens. It has a brushed stainless steel body and non-stick cooking pot, which can be washed in the dishwasher. It has a browning option for searing meat, and a steaming rack. If you don't want to start dinner until later, it has a programmable timer up to 8 hours.

Chapter 6 - Converting Stove Top Pressure Cooker Recipes to Electric Ones

Converting the recipes you use for stove top pressure cookers to electric pressure cookers is a lot easier than converting slow cooker recipes. The main difference between stovetop recipes and electric ones is how long it takes to cook the food. Because electric pressure cookers don't have the high PSI like stove top ones do, recipes take longer. Many recipe books specifically for pressure cookers include a range of time, with the longer time intended for electric pressure cookers. There is no specific formula you can apply to a stove top recipe to get the time for electric, but I have intended a time chart in Index 1 of this book for your convenience.

Because electrics take longer, they require more liquid at the beginning of the recipe, since more liquid gets evaporated with the longer time. If the cooker doesn't have enough liquid, it will usually shut off. Look at the manual for your specific electric cooker and see what the minimum liquid requirement is. It is usually 1 ½ -2 cups.

> **Cooking Tip**
> When the electric pressure cooker is going to run for *more* than 10 minutes, you'll need to put in 2 cups of liquid.

If the stove top recipe says "preheat," you can use your electric cooker's "brown" or "sauté" setting to warm the cooker up in addition to actual sautéing. You can also use either of those two settings when you're bringing something to a boil before locking the lid and starting the pressure program.

When it comes time to lock the lid, a lot of electric cookers do this automatically once you've selected the pressure program. If it doesn't, you just twist the lid and check to make sure the lid and valve are set to "seal" or "pressure." Electric cookers won't start until the lid is sealed, so if you're afraid the cooker might start and the lid isn't on all the way, that's impossible. Another nice thing about electric cookers is when a stove top recipe says to turn the heat up or down to maintain pressure, that doesn't apply to electrics. The heating element and microprocessor deal with that on their own, so you don't have to touch the cooker while it does its thing.

If the stove top recipe says to release pressure, it will say to either do it manually, naturally, or under cold water. With an electric cooker, you can only release pressure the first two ways. For manual or quick-release, turn the lid valve to "open" or "release." For a natural release, turn off the electric pressure cooker and wait. Some recipes will call for a combination of pressure-release methods, such as a natural release for 10 minutes, and then a quick-release.

For a guide on how to convert slow cooker recipes to pressure cookers, look to Index 2.

Chapter 7 - Breakfasts

Lemon-Blueberry Oats

Serves: 5
Time: 28 minutes (10 minute cook time)

Steel-cut oats are a filling, nutritious grain that has been shown to increase heart health. The fiber in steel-cut oats can also help with weight loss. A pressure cooker cooks steel-cut oats in only 10 minutes, and when mixed with succulent blueberries, bright lemon zest, and chia seeds, you get delicious oatmeal that tastes like blueberry-lemon bread.

Ingredients:
3 cups water
1 cup steel-cut oats
1 cup fresh blueberries
½ cup half & half
¼ cup chia seeds
2 tablespoons sugar
1 tablespoon butter
1 tablespoon lemon zest
¼ teaspoon salt

Directions:
1. Melt the butter on the Sauté setting in your electric pressure cooker.
2. When melted, add the oats and stir for about 3 minutes, until they are nice and toasty.
3. Pour in the water, sugar, salt, lemon zest, and half & half, and stir.
4. Secure the pressure cooker lid and cook on 10 minutes on high pressure.

5. Once time is up, turn off the pressure cooker and let the pressure decrease naturally for 10 minutes. Quick-release any leftover pressure.
6. Stir in the blueberries and chia seeds.
7. Without turning the pressure cooker on, put the lid back on and let the oats thicken for 5 minutes.
8. Serve with optional add-ins, like honey, maple syrup, nuts, or milk.

Nutritional information (per serving):
Calories - 225
Protein- 7
Carbs - 37
Fat - 6
Fiber - 5

Pressure-Cooker Quiche w/ Sausage, Ham, and Bacon

Serves: 4
Time: 40 minutes (30 minute cook time)

Cooking Tip
For lifting containers in and out of the cooker, you can make a "sling" out of a wide strip of foil. Place the dish on top of this strip, fold the ends of the strip up, and lift to raise the dish.

Quiche is prime comfort food, especially when it's full of meat like ground sausage, ham, and crumbled bacon. The eggs become a perfect, fluffy, almost custard-like carrier for cozy flavors like green onions and of course, cheese. This recipe cuts out a few carbs by not having a crust, and it's also acceptable if you're gluten-free.

Ingredients:
6 beaten eggs
2 chopped green onions
1 cup cooked ground sausage
1 cup shredded cheddar cheese
4 slices cooked, crumbled bacon
½ cup chopped ham
½ cup milk
Salt and pepper

Directions:
1. Pour 1 ½ cups of water into your electric pressure cooker.
2. Set the trivet inside the cooker.
3. In a big bowl, mix eggs, milk, pepper, and salt.
4. In a pressure-cooker safe dish (like a 1-quart soufflé dish), combine the crumbled bacon, sausage, chopped onions, chopped ham, and cheese.
5. Pour the eggs over the soufflé dish and stir.
6. Cover the dish with foil.
7. Put dish into the cooker so it sits on the trivet.
8. Secure the lid and cook on high pressure for 30 minutes.
9. When the timer goes off, turn off the pressure cooker and let the pressure decrease naturally for 10 minutes.
10. Quick-release the remaining pressure.
11. Lift the dish out of the cooker and take off the foil.

12.   Serve hot!

Nutritional information (per serving):
Calories - 409
Protein- 30
Carbs - 3
Fat - 33
Fiber - 0

Classic French-Baked Eggs

Serves: 4
Time: About 6 minutes (4 minute cook time)

French-baked eggs are a classic recipe, where a chef cracks an egg in a ramekin, adds cheese or cream, and bakes it all in an oven. It is a versatile dish that is traditionally served with ingredients like ham, gruyere cheese, and chives. There's really no wrong way to dress up these eggs, however. You can substitute in smoked salmon, cream cheese, and capers, or keep things meat-free with a fresh tomato slice, mozzarella, and basil.

Ingredients:
4 eggs
4 slices of ham (or any other meat or veggie)
4 slices of cheese (or your choice, or a splash of cream)
Chives, parsley, or any other fresh herb
Olive oil

Directions:
1.   Pour one cup of water into your electric pressure cooker and set the trivet inside.
2.   Smear olive oil on the insides of four ramekins, so the food doesn't get stuck.

3. Put a slice of ham in the ramekin, and then break an egg inside.
4. Add cheese.
5. Wrap the ramekins in foil. If you want a soft egg yolk, wrap the foil tightly.
6. Put the four ramekins in the steamer basket and put on top of the trivet in the pressure cooker.
7. Secure the lid and cook on low pressure for 4 minutes.
8. When the timer goes off, do a quick-release.
9. Serve right away and enjoy!

Nutritional information (per serving):
Calories - 240
Protein- 19
Carbs - 2
Fat - 17
Fiber - 0

Autumn Apple-Cherry Risotto
Serves: 6
Time: 13 minutes (6 minute cook time)

Risotto for breakfast? Absolutely! This sweet take on arborio rice features delicious autumn flavors like apple and cinnamon, along with dried cherries, which are full of vitamin A and copper. The recipe only takes 13 minutes from start to finish, and you have breakfast for six people.

Ingredients:
3 cups of milk
1 ½ cups arborio rice
2 cored and diced apples
1 cup apple juice
2 tablespoons butter

½ cup dried cherries
⅓cup brown sugar
1 ½ teaspoons cinnamon
¼ teaspoon salt

Directions:
1. Melt the butter on the Sauté setting in your electric pressure cooker.
2. Add the rice and cook for about 3-4 minutes. Remember to stir so the rice doesn't burn.
3. Next, add in the cinnamon, salt, brown sugar, and apples.
4. Pour in the juice and milk and stir.
5. Secure the pressure cooker lid and cook on high pressure for 6 minutes.
6. When the timer goes off, turn the cooker off and quick-release the pressure.
7. When the pressure is all the way down, take off the lid and add the dried cherries.
8. Serve right away with a sprinkle of brown sugar or more milk.

Nutritional information (per serving):
Calories - 287
Protein- 10
Carbs - 55
Fat - 6
Fiber - 5

Homemade Bread w/ 2-Ingredient Strawberry Jam
Serves: 8
Time: 1 hour (20-25 minutes cook time for bread, 2 minutes for jam)

Did you know you can make soft bread that rivals store-bought bread, all in an electric pressure cooker? You will need something like a stainless-steel tea canister, or a 400g aluminum powdered milk can with the inner-lip part taken out. This will serve as your loaf "pan." To go with your fresh bread, you can make a quick strawberry jam in the electric pressure cooker, so the whole two recipes only take about one hour (not counting any clean-up).

Ingredients:
2 cups all-purpose flour
1 ¼ cup whole-milk plain yogurt
1 teaspoon olive oil
½ teaspoon baking soda
1 teaspoon salt
2 pounds cored and halved strawberries
1 ½ pounds light, mild honey

Directions:
1. Take your bread container and rub in one teaspoon of olive oil.
2. In a mixing bowl, combine the salt, baking soda, and flour.
3. Add the yogurt and stir.
4. Knead until the dough holds together and feels slightly sticky. If it's still too flaky, add a bit of water.
5. Knead until everything is mixed.
6. Stretch out the dough and lower it into your bread container. Add a drop of oil to the top of the dough, since you will be covering it in foil, and don't want the dough to stick.
7. Cover with foil, leaving a little room for the dough to rise out of the container.

8. Tie a piece of kitchen string around the edge of the foil, so the foil stays on tightly.
9. Put the container into the steamer rack and lower into the pressure cooker.
10. Pour in just enough hot water so half of the container is submerged.
11. Secure the lid and cook on high pressure for 20-25 minutes.
12. When the timer goes off, turn off the pressure cooker and let the pressure go down naturally.
13. When the pressure is all gone, open the pressure cooker and take out the container.
14. If a toothpick comes out clean, the bread is ready.
15. Take it out of the container and let it sit on a cooling rack for 10 minutes before cutting.

To make the jam:
1. Pour the strawberries into the pressure cooker and add honey.
2. Turn the pressure cooker on to its "Warm" setting and stir until the honey has liquefied.
3. Turn the pressure cooker to sauté (or brown) and stir until the jam begins to boil.
4. Immediately secure the pressure cooker lid and cook on high pressure for 2 minutes.
5. When the timer goes off, turn off the cooker and let the pressure decrease naturally.
6. When the pressure is gone, take off the lid and turn the cooker back to sauté or brown until the jam has begun to boil again and reaches 220-degrees F.
7. Pour into just-washed jars and screw on the jar tops.
8. Store in the fridge for 4-6 weeks. You get about two pints total.

Calories - 144
Protein- 4
Carbs - 26
Fat - 2
Fiber - 1

Classic Grits

Serves: 3-4
Time: 30 minutes (15 minute cook time)

Grits are a classic Southern fare, and great for breakfast on cold mornings. The coarse ground grits become like a savory oatmeal with butter and cheese. Getting the texture right can be tricky, but with an electric pressure cooker, it's super easy.

Ingredients:
1 cup coarse ground grits
1 cup shredded cheese
3 cups water
2 tablespoons butter
Salt and pepper

Directions:
1. Add the minimum amount of water required for your electric pressure cooker.
2. In a bowl, mix grits, 2 ½ cups of water, and the butter.
3. Put the bowl on top of the trivet inside the pressure cooker.
4. Secure the lid and cook on high pressure for 15 minutes.
5. When the timer beeps, turn off the pressure cooker and let the pressure decrease naturally.
6. When the pressure is all the way down, take out the bowl of grits.

7. Stir, and then add the cheese. Stir again.
8. Season to taste with salt and pepper.
9. Serve and enjoy!

Nutritional information (1 cup):
Calories - 282
Protein- 13
Carbs - 26
Fat - 13.7
Fiber - .5

Peaches 'N Cream Oats
Serves: 4
Time: 13 minutes (3 minute cook time)

This sweet steel-cut oatmeal is not only delicious, it's vegan! Instead of cow milk, it uses creamy coconut milk, and is sweetened with vanilla instead of honey. This is a perfect breakfast for the summer when peaches are ripe and fresh.

Ingredients:
2 cups water
1 cup steel-cut oats
1 cup full-fat coconut milk
2 diced peaches
½ of a scraped vanilla bean

Directions:
1. Throw everything into the electric pressure cooker and stir.
2. Secure the lid and cook on high pressure for 3 minutes.
3. When the timer goes off, turn off the cooker and let the pressure go down naturally.
4. Serve with your favorite vegan sweetener or eat as is.

Nutritional information (per serving):
Calories - 172
Protein- 3
Carbs - 16
Fat - 12
Fiber – 4

Millet Pudding w/ Coconut and Lime

Serves: 4
Time: 22 minutes (12 minute cook time)

Millet is an underrated grain. It's high-protein and low-carb, like quinoa, and cooks extremely quickly. This breakfast pudding is a unique and tasty twist on traditional oatmeal, complete with coconut milk, lime, and vanilla. Millet has been shown to cause health issues if you have blood sugar problems, so eat this seed in moderation and consult your doctor.

Ingredients:
13.5-ounce can coconut milk
1 cup water
⅔cup millet
Lime zest
½ teaspoon vanilla
¼ cup toasted coconut

Directions:
1.   Put the coconut milk, water, millet, a little salt, and vanilla into the electric pressure cooker.
2.   Lock the cover.
3.   Cook on high pressure for 12 minutes.
4.   When the timer goes off, turn off the pressure cooker and let the pressure go down on its own.

5. Stir in the lime zest and top with the toasted coconut. Sweeten with honey, maple syrup, or another sweetener of your choice.

<u>Nutritional information (per serving):</u>
Calories - 177
Protein- 4
Carbs - 31
Fat - 4
Fiber - 1.5

Pressure-Cooker Soft-Boiled Eggs

Serves: 6
Time: 5 minutes (1 minute cook time)

Eggs are the perfect breakfast food. They're quick, packed with healthy protein and fat, and versatile. This recipe tells you how to soft-boil eggs that go best with a slice of toasted whole-grain bread and a crack of fresh black pepper. It's a simple breakfast, but a delicious one.

<u>Ingredients:</u>
6 fresh eggs
Water
6 slices whole-grain bread
Black pepper
Salt

<u>Directions:</u>
1. Pour one cup of water into your electric pressure cooker.
2. Place six eggs in the steamer basket and lower into the cooker.
3. Select low pressure and cook for 1 minute.

4. Quick-release the pressure.
5. While the eggs cool, toast your bread and plate.
6. Carefully unpeel the eggs.
7. The eggs will run, so cut over the bread.
8. Sprinkle with salt and black pepper to taste.

Nutritional information (per serving):
Calories - 180
Protein- 11
Carbs - 19
Fat - 7
Fiber - 1.9

Bacon Hash Browns

Serves: 4
Time: 25 minutes (15 minute cook time)

Hash Browns are a real breakfast treat. They have a warm, crunchy exterior that give way to a tender inside. With these hashbrowns, the insides are also flecked with bacon and seasoned with fresh parsley. These are great as an accompaniment to eggs or sausage.

Ingredients:
2 pounds of washed and peeled russet potatoes
8-ounces of crumbled bacon
2 tablespoons olive oil
2 tablespoons chopped parsley
Salt and pepper

Directions:
1. Run the potatoes through a food processor, or grate them into long strips.
2. Rinse in a strainer and dry well.

3. Heat the olive oil in your pressure cooker on the sauté setting.
4. Put in your potatoes and season with salt and pepper.
5. Sauté for 5-6 minutes.
6. Once they're browned, add the parsley and bacon.
7. Press down on the potato-bacon-parsley mixture with a spatula.
8. Secure the pressure cooker and cook on low pressure for 6-7 minutes.
9. Quick-release the pressure.
10. Serve right away!

Nutritional information (per serving):
Calories - 575
Protein- 38
Carbs - 35
Fat - 40
Fiber - 5

Chapter 8 - Soups and Stews

Sausage Lentil Soup
Serves: 6-8
Time: 20 minutes (15 minute cook time)

This high-protein soup uses pre-cooked sausage to keep the cooking time short, and a colorful mix of roasted tomatoes, carrots, celery, and onions for the veggies. Lentils, which are a type of bean, are known for their high protein, fiber, and easy digestibility.

Ingredients:
6 cups water
4 minced garlic cloves
1-2 cups chopped, cooked sausage
2 bay leaves
2 cups beef broth
2 cups crushed tomatoes
1 cup chopped celery, carrots, and onions
¾ cup dried lentils
Salt and pepper

Directions:
1. Brown (or sauté) the celery, carrots, and onion mix, and garlic until they become fragrant.
2. Turn off the sauté setting and add everything else to the electric pressure cooker.
3. Shut the pressure cooker lid and cook on high for 15 minutes.
4. Quick-release the pressure.
5. Open the lid and stir.
6. Season with salt and pepper.
7. Serve with sour cream or yogurt!

Cooking Tip
If you want the soup to be thicker, mix some broth with flour to make a roux, and then add it to the pot.

Nutritional information (per serving):
Calories - 313.9
Protein- 14.7
Carbs - 16.6
Fat - 21.1
Fiber - 5.8

Lamb Curry
Serves: 8
Time: 55 minutes (25 minute cook time)

Lamb is not a frequently-used meat, depending on your culture, so lots of people aren't sure how to cook it. A curry is the perfect platform, and the pressure cooker allows the meat to turn out deliciously-tender and spiced with ginger, garlic, and cinnamon.

Ingredients:
2 ½ pounds lamb shoulder, cut into 1-inch pieces
4 cups packed spinach leaves
2 cups chicken broth
12 ounces of fingerling potatoes
6 minced garlic cloves
3 tablespoons grated fresh ginger
2 chopped onions
3 tablespoons safflower oil
1 cinnamon stick
2 crushed cardamom pods

2 ¼ teaspoons cumin seeds

2 teaspoons tomato paste

1 ½ teaspoons crushed coriander seeds

¾ teaspoon ground turmeric

Sea salt

Directions:
1. Begin by heating the oil in your pressure cooker.
2. Sauté the garlic, ginger, onions, and 1 teaspoon of salt for about 3 minutes.
3. Throw in the seasonings, including the cinnamon stick, and cook for 30 seconds.
4. Add the tomato paste and stir for another 15 seconds.
5. Pour in the broth and add the potatoes and lamb. Season.
6. Close the pressure cooker lid and cook on high pressure for 25 minutes.
7. Quick-release the pressure.
8. Medium-done lamb will be at 160-degrees.
9. Stir in the spinach before serving.

Nutritional information (per serving):

Calories - 314

Protein- 26

Carbs - 10

Fat – 19

Fiber - 1

White Chicken Chili

Serves: 10

Time: 1 hour, 20 minutes (60 minute cook time)

This broth-based chicken chili is a lighter alternative to hearty beef chili. It's great for cooler nights, and even better for leftovers. For heat, you have green chilies, 2 jalapenos, and two kinds of ground peppers (cayenne and paprika). If you aren't a fan of spicy, just use one Jalapeno and ease up on the pepper.

Ingredients:
8 cups chicken broth
1 pound rinsed dried Great Northern beans
3 cups cooked chicken
4 minced garlic cloves
1 cup whole milk
1 sliced onion
2 cans chopped green chilies
2 sliced Jalapenos
2 tablespoons butter
2 tablespoons cornmeal
1 ½ tablespoons ground cumin
½ teaspoon paprika
½ teaspoon cayenne pepper
White pepper and salt
Olive oil

Directions:
1. Chop up all the veggies (chilies, Jalapenos, garlic, and onions) and sauté with olive oil and 2 tablespoons for 5 minutes.
2. Turn off the pressure cooker so it doesn't keep browning.
3. Add in the beans and mix.
4. Pour in the chicken broth.
5. Lock the lid and set to high pressure for 60 minutes.

6. When the beeper sounds, let the pressure go down on its own.
7. Open the lid carefully and stir.
8. Add the seasonings and chicken, and let everything cool for 10 minutes.
9. Simmer for a few minutes.
10. To thicken the chili, mix a half cup of milk with 1 tablespoon of cornmeal.
11. Add to pot and simmer for 5-10 minutes until the flavors have blended.
12. Season again if necessary.
13. Serve with your favorite topping, like shredded cheese, herbs, or sour cream!

Nutritional information (per serving) (1 cup serving):
Calories - 358
Protein- 46
Carbs - 33
Fat - 2
Fiber - 7

Beef Chili in 15-Minutes

Serves: 5-6
Time: 15 minutes (4 minute cook time)

This chili actually only cooks for 4 minutes, so the name of this recipe is an overstatement. While white chicken chili is perfect for cool nights, beef chili is the stew of choice when it's really chilly outside. The hearty meat and spices warm a body right up, and it makes great leftovers, because the flavors get to steep even longer.

Ingredients:
2 pounds lean beef

½ pound chopped chorizo
2 cups chopped onion
½ cup water
15-ounces of diced tomatoes
1 chopped, seeded green bell pepper
1-2 pressed garlic cloves
3-4 tablespoons chili powder
1 ½ tablespoons unsweetened cocoa powder
1 tablespoon olive oil
2 teaspoons whole cumin seeds
1 teaspoon dried oregano
Salt and pepper

Directions:
1. Turn your cooker on "sauté" and heat the olive oil.
2. Add cumin seeds and stir until toasty for 20 seconds.
3. Put in the meat gradually and stirring between each batch to break up the meat.
4. Cook until the meat is browned.
5. Add water and onions.
6. Deglaze the pot.

Cooking Tip
"Deglazing" is when you add a cooking liquid (like water, broth, or wine) to a pot and scrape off the bits of food that have stuck to the sides. These burned or browned bits add flavor.

7. Pour in the cocoa and chili powder, followed by the pepper and chorizo.
8. Pour in the tomatoes, and do not stir.

9. Secure the pressure cooker lid and cook on high pressure for 4 minutes.
10. Quick-release the pressure when time is up.
11. Mix in the pressed garlic, oregano, and salt and pepper.
12. If you want more heat, add in 1 tablespoon chili powder.
13. With the lid off, continue to simmer for 3-5 minutes so all the flavors mingle.
14. Serve with your favorite chili topping.

Nutritional information (per serving) (1 cup serving):
Calories - 270
Protein- 23
Carbs - 28
Fat - 8
Fiber - 0

Lasagna Soup with Ricotta Balls
Serves: 4-6
Time: 25 minutes (10 minute cook time)

Lasagna is a favorite comfort food, but it's very high in carbs. To make it more acceptable, just make this soup! It has all the great flavors of lasagna, but in a less messy, lower-calorie package. You even get to make rich, delicious ricotta balls that rest in the soup bowl.

Ingredients:
4 cups chicken broth
2 pounds spicy Italian sausage
32-ounces of chopped tomatoes
1 chopped yellow onion
3 minced garlic cloves
1 package Mafalda pasta
2 tablespoons Italian seasoning

2-3 tablespoons fresh ricotta
Shredded mozzarella

Directions:
1. Heat up the olive oil using the "sauté" setting.
2. Add meat and crumble it up using a spatula.
3. Once brown, add the Italian seasoning and turn off the pressure cooker.
4. Stir in the garlic, chopped onions, and tomatoes.
5. Add the broth.
6. Secure the pressure cooker lid and cook on high for 10 minutes. You can also use the "Soup" setting.
7. While that cooks, make the cheese balls.
8. Mix 2-3 tablespoons with as much mozzarella as you want (bearing in mind calorie count) and roll into a tight ball.
9. Put in the fridge until you're ready to eat.
10. When the pressure cooker timer goes off, quick-release the pressure.
11. Stir well.
12. Add 1-2 cups of pasta.
13. Close the pressure cooker lid and cook for 1 minute.
14. Let the pressure go down naturally before opening and serving.

Nutritional information (per serving):
Calories - 557
Protein- 34
Carbs - 52
Fat - 23
Fiber - 4

Barley-and-Portobello Soup
Serves: 6-8

Time: 30 minutes (25 minute cook time)

This is one of the healthiest soups you could have on a cold autumn or winter evening. It is packed with vegetables like carrots, mushrooms, and celery, and pearled barley, which is a nutritious whole-grain. It's low in calories and fat, and a great alternative to chicken noodle soup if you're feeling a bit under the weather.

Ingredients:
4 cups water
3 cups chicken broth
3 diced celery stalks
2 minced garlic cloves
2 diced carrots
2 sliced portobello mushrooms, large
1 diced tomato
½ diced yellow onion
¾ cup rinsed and drained dry pearled barley
2 thyme sprigs
Olive oil
Salt and pepper

Directions:
1. Pour a splash of olive oil in your electric pressure cooker and heat on the "sauté" setting.
2. Add the onion and garlic and sauté until they become fragrant.
3. Toss in the carrots and celery, and sauté for 5 minutes.
4. Next, add the tomato, mushrooms, barley, chicken broth, water, and sprigs of thyme.
5. Close the pressure cooker and cook for 25 minutes on high pressure, or select the "Soup" setting.

6. When time is up, unplug the cooker and let the pressure come down on its own.
7. Season to taste with salt and pepper.
8. Serve hot!

Nutritional information (per serving) (1 cup):
Calories - 73
Protein- 1.9
Carbs - 11.7
Fat - 2.3
Fiber - 0.7

Chicken Corn Chowder with Pumpkin
Serves: 4-5
Time: About 10 minutes (4 minute cook time)

Sweet corn, tender chicken, and creamy pumpkin are the stars of this soup. You also get rich flavors from the garlic, onion, and cubed potatoes, which help add some heft to this hearty dish. Nutmeg and red pepper flakes are also sprinkled in to add some great spice to compliment the pumpkin.

Ingredients:
2 14.5 cans of chicken broth
2 uncooked, diced chicken breasts
2 cubed russet potatoes
2 cups frozen corn
1 15-ounce can of pumpkin puree
1 minced garlic clove
1 cup diced onion
½ cup Half & Half
2 tablespoons butter
½ teaspoon Italian seasoning
¼ teaspoon black pepper

⅛ teaspoon nutmeg
⅛ teaspoon red pepper flakes

Directions:
1. Melt the butter in the pressure cooker.
2. Add the onion and sauté for 5 minutes, until the onion becomes clear.
3. Add the garlic and sauté for another minute.
4. Combine the broth, pumpkin, and seasonings in the pot.
5. Lastly, put in the diced chicken and potatoes.
6. Secure the pressure cooker lid and cook on high pressure for 4 minutes.
7. Turn off the pressure cooker and quick-release the pressure.
8. Add the Half & Half and corn. Stir.
9. Season with salt and pepper.
10. Serve with some fresh, chopped parsley if desired.

Nutritional information (2 cups):
Calories - 321
Protein- 19.4
Carbs - 36
Fat - 13
Fiber - 4.4

Zuppa Toscana
Serves: 8
Time: About 18 minutes (4 minute cook time)

Literally translated as, "soup in the style of Tuscany," this dish is best known as one of The Olive Garden's staples. Here, however, it is a bit healthier and lighter on the fat and salt. Instead of heavy cream, you use evaporated milk. If you want a spicier soup, or one that's less spicy, simply adjust the amount of red pepper flakes.

Ingredients:
6 diced slices of bacon
3 cubed russet potatoes
1 pound ground chicken sausage
3 14.5-ounce cans of chicken broth
1 12-ounce can of evaporated milk
2 cups chopped spinach
1 cup of diced onion
1 cup shredded parmesan cheese
3 minced garlic cloves
3 tablespoons cornstarch
1 tablespoon butter
½ teaspoon black pepper
½ teaspoon salt
⅛ teaspoon red pepper flakes

Directions:
1. Sauté the bacon in your electric pressure cooker.
2. When crisp, take them out of the pot and fold in paper towels.
3. Brown the chicken sausage in the pressure cooker, and then like the bacon, put on a plate with paper towels.
4. Melt the butter in the pot.
5. Add the onion and cook for 5 minutes until they become tender.
6. Add the garlic and cook for another minute.
7. Pour in 1 can of broth and seasonings.

8. Put the diced potatoes into the steamer basket and lower into the cooker.
9. Secure the lid and cook on high pressure for 4 minutes.
10. When the time is up, quick-release the pressure.
11. Pour in the other 2 cans of broth.
12. In another bowl, mix the cornstarch in with some evaporated milk until dissolved.
13. Pour in this mixture along with the rest of the evaporated milk.
14. Simmer until the soup becomes to boil.
15. When the soup is thickened, add ¾ cup of cheese, the spinach, sausage, potatoes, and three slices of the bacon.
16. Top with the rest of the bacon and cheese, and serve!

Nutritional information (per serving):
Calories - 233
Protein- 9
Carbs - 18.5
Fat - 14.3
Fiber - 2.4

Simple 'n Quick Miso Soup
Serves: 4
Time: 7 minutes (6 minute cook time)

Miso soup comes from Japan, and is a great option for vegetarians and vegans alike. It's also great for people following a macrobiotic diet, which shuns processed foods and favors whole-grains and veggies. Miso soup can be eaten any time of day, including breakfast, and one serving equals less than 50 calories.

Ingredients:

4 cups water
1 cup cubed firm, silken tofu
2 chopped carrots
2 chopped celery stalks
1 small onion, in half-moon slices
½ cup fresh corn
2 tablespoons miso paste
1 teaspoon wakame flakes
Soy sauce

Cooking Tip
Wakame flakes are sweet seaweed and can be found at any Asian market or more upscale grocery stores, like Whole Foods. You can also find them at some Walmarts.

Directions:
1. Mix all the ingredients (except the miso paste and soy sauce) in the pressure cooker pot.
2. Secure the lid and cook at high pressure for 6 minutes.
3. When the timer beeps, quick-release the pressure.
4. Pour about one cup of broth into a bowl and dissolve the miso paste in it.
5. Pour back into the pressure cooker and stir to combine the flavors.
6. Serve hot with soy sauce.

Nutritional information (per serving):
Calories - 46
Protein- 3.8
Carbs - 3.7

Fat - 1.7
Fiber - 1

Moroccan Red Lentil Soup

Serves: 4
Time: 18 minutes (8 minute cook time)

Red lentils are the main event of this dish. They are an excellent source of protein, iron, and fiber, while staying low in fat and calories. Celery, onions, and potatoes round out the rest of this soup, and a cup of wheat berries adds some whole grains to the party.

Ingredients:
8 cups of water
1 pound of red lentils
6 peeled and diced plum tomatoes
4 sliced celery stalks
4 minced garlic cloves
2 peeled and diced potatoes
2 chopped onions
1 cup cooked wheat berries
1 tablespoon olive oil
1 tablespoon tomato paste
1 bay leaf
2 teaspoons salt
1 teaspoon turmeric
1 teaspoon cumin
1 teaspoon pepper
1 teaspoon cinnamon
¼ teaspoon ground ginger
1 pinch saffron

Directions:

1. Set your electric pressure cooker to sauté and heat the olive oil.
2. Add the onion and garlic until fragrant.
3. Next, add the celery and cook until they've become soft.
4. Toss in 1 teaspoon of salt and the other spices and sauté for another minute or so.
5. Add in the potatoes, lentils, tomato paste, and water.
6. Secure the lid and cook on high pressure for 8 minutes, or on the "soup" setting.
7. When the cycle is over, unplug the pressure cooker and quick-release the pressure.
8. Stir in the remaining salt, cooked wheat berries, and tomatoes.
9. Let it simmer until those ingredients are hot and combined into the soup.
10. Serve and enjoy!

Nutritional information (per serving):
Calories - 152
Protein- 9
Carbs - 28
Fat - 1
Fiber - 9

Butternut Squash Bisque

Serves: 6
Time: About 15 minutes (12 minute cook time)

Butternut squash is one of my favorite vegetables. It is so sweet, smooth, and this pureed soup is the perfect vehicle for it. Spices like ginger, nutmeg, and pure maple syrup are amazing compliments to the squash's natural mild flavor, while tart Granny Smith apples help add some acid and tanginess.

Ingredients:

2 peeled and cubed butternut squashes
5 cups chicken stock
3 peeled and cut Granny Smith apples
2 cups kale
2 peeled and cut onions
1 pint Half & Half
2 tablespoons pure maple syrup
1 tablespoon olive oil
2 teaspoons ground ginger
2 teaspoons ground cumin
½ teaspoon nutmeg
Salt

Cooking Tip
Depending on the thickness you want, you can use heavy cream for thicker soup, or milk for a thinner consistency.

Directions:
1. Heat olive oil in your electric pressure cooker on the "sauté" setting.
2. Add onions and cook until they become translucent and soft.
3. Add the rest of the ingredients (except the maple syrup, Half & Half, and salt).
4. Secure the pressure cooker lid and cook on high pressure for 12 minutes.
5. Turn off the cooker and quick-release the pressure.
6. Open the lid and cool for a few minutes before blending.
7. Add the Half & Half, salt, and maple syrup.

8. Use a handheld blender or regular blender to puree.
9. Season again with salt if necessary and serve warm.

Nutritional information (per serving):
Calories - 140
Protein- 1.7
Carbs - 17.8
Fat - 8
Fiber - 3.1

Julia Child's French Onion Soup (Electric Pressure Cooker Version)

Serves: 6-7
Time: 35 minutes (6 minute cook time)

Julia Child's recipes are often known for their complexity, but this version of her French onion soup is a little simpler when you make it in a pressure cooker. It is also a lot faster, and the whole thing takes about 35 minutes.

Ingredients:
5 thinly-sliced big yellow onions
6 cups meat stock
1 tablespoon butter
1 tablespoon olive oil
1 teaspoon salt
¼ teaspoon sugar
½ cup dry white wine
¼ grated onion wedge
3 tablespoons Cognac

Roux:
4 tablespoons butter
¼ cup flour

Directions:

1. Heat the butter and oil in your pressure cooker.
2. Add the onions and sauté until they become clear.
3. Turn off the cooker and add the sugar and salt.
4. Stir until the onions are browned.
5. In a separate pan, make the roux by adding the butter and flour (in equal amounts) and stirring on medium heat until the butter melts and flour foams.
6. Keep stirring until it has become tan.
7. Set the roux aside.
8. With the white wine, deglaze the pressure cooker.
9. Add the meat stock and secure the pressure cooker lid.
10. Cook on high pressure for 6 minutes.
11. Quick-release the pressure.
12. Season with salt and pepper.
13. Spoon out some of the soup and add to the roux to combine.
14. Pour the soup and roux back into the pressure cooker and simmer uncovered.
15. Turn off the cooker and add the Cognac and grated onion wedge.
16. Serve up the soup in bowls and sprinkle with shredded gruyere cheese.
17. For the bread topping, cover the soup with toasted slices of French Bread, cover with more cheese, and then put in the broiler for 2-3 minutes.

Nutritional information (per serving):

Calories - 439

Protein- 23

Carbs - 30

Fat - 22.7

Fiber - 2.3

Meat Entrees

Pork

Apples & Onions Pork Tenderloin

Serves: 5-6
Time: 80 minutes (60 minute cook time)

Pork and apples go great together. The sweetness of the apples bring out the flavor of the pork, and when you combine those two with onion, you get a mix of sweet, acidic, and luscious flavors. You don't have to worry about dry pork in a pressure cooker - it practically melts.

Ingredients:
4 pounds of pork rump
3 sliced apples
2 cups apple juice
1 cup chicken broth
2 bay leaves
1 sliced onion
Salt and pepper

Directions:
1. Trim fat from the pork and season on both sides with salt and pepper.
2. Put the onions and apples into the pressure cooker and pour the broth and apple juice over.
3. Lastly, add the pork.
4. Close the pressure cooker lid and cook for 60 minutes on high pressure.
5. Let the pressure decrease naturally when the timer goes off.

6.   Cut up the pork and pour over the apple-onion gravy!

Nutritional information (per serving):
Calories - 215
Protein- 23
Carbs - 15
Fat - 7
Fiber - 3

Pork Chops & Cabbage
Serves: 4
Time: 20 minutes (8 minute cook time)

This recipe is based on a Tuscany pork dish and uses regular ol' cabbage and some thick pork chops. Just throw everything in the cooker and in less than half an hour (including prep), you have a hearty meal.

Ingredients:
Four ¾-inch pork chops
¾ cup chicken stock
1 pound cabbage
1 tablespoon veggie oil
2 teaspoons flour
1 teaspoon salt
1 teaspoon fennel seeds
1 teaspoon pepper

Directions:
1.   Season pork chops with salt, pepper, and fennel.
2.   Slice the cabbage in half and then in ¾ inch slices.
3.   Heat the oil in the pressure cooker.
4.   Brown the pork on one side and then remove.

5. Add the cabbage slices, and then the pork chops, with the unbrowned side down.
6. Pour the meat stock around the pressure cooker edges.
7. Secure the lid and cook for 8 minutes on high pressure.
8. When time is up, let the pressure come down on its own.
9. Move the pork chops and cabbage and cover.
10. Bring the cooking liquid to a boil in the cooker and add the flour to thicken.
11. Pour this gravy on top of the pork and cabbage before serving.

Nutritional information (per serving):
Calories - 147
Protein- 16
Carbs - 8
Fat - 6
Fiber - 2.8

Simple Braised Pork
Serves: 8
Time: 60 minutes (50 minute cook time)

With just a handful of ingredients, you can turn pork butt into the star of the dinner table. This recipe takes a little longer than some of the other ones, but there's little to no prep, and of course, it's still way faster than any other cooking method.

Ingredients:
5 pounds cubed pork butt, ½ inches
2 cups chicken stock
2 cups red wine
½ cup lemon juice
¼ cup minced onion

¼ cup garlic powder
2 tablespoons olive oil

Directions:
1.   Add the pork, olive oil, onion, garlic, and paprika into the pressure cooker and mix until coated.
2.   Pour in the lemon juice, red wine, and enough stock to submerge the pork.
3.   Secure the lid.
4.   Cook on high pressure for about 50 minutes.
5.   Wait 15 minutes before opening the cooker and serving.

Nutritional information (per serving):
Calories - 754.6
Protein- 55.7
Carbs - 9.2
Fat - 48.8
Fiber - .9

Pressure-Cooker Pork Vindaloo
Serves: 6
Time: 1 ½ hours (35 minute cook time)

A vindaloo is an Indian dish made with meat, curry, and other spices. This recipe is for a pork variation, and includes easy-to-get seasonings like garlic, cumin, cloves, and paprika. No need to find an Indian market and dig through spices you've never heard of, though there's another time for that kind of adventure.

Ingredients:
3 pounds boneless pork roast, cut into 1-inch pieces
3 chopped onions
8 minced garlic cloves

1 cup chicken broth

1 (14.5-ounce) can of diced tomatoes

¼ cup minced cilantro

¼ cup flour

2 tablespoons veggie oil

2 tablespoons red wine vinegar

1 tablespoon paprika

1 tablespoon mustard seeds

1 teaspoon ground cumin

1 teaspoon sugar

¼ teaspoon cayenne pepper

⅛ teaspoon ground cloves

Directions:

1. Pat the pork dry before seasoning with salt and pepper.
2. In your pressure cooker, heat 1 tablespoon oil until it begins to smoke.
3. Brown half of the meat on both sides for about 8 minutes.
4. Remove the meat.
5. Add another tablespoon oil and sauté the onions with some salt for 5 minutes, or until softened.
6. Add the mustard seeds, paprika, cumin, cloves, cayenne, and garlic and cook until they become fragrant.
7. Whisk in the flour to cook for 1 minute.
8. Pour in the broth and deglaze the pot.
9. Next, add the vinegar, sugar, tomatoes, browned pork, and unbrowned pork.
10. Secure the pressure cooker lid and cook on high for 35 minutes.
11. When ready, turn off the cooker and wait for the pressure to come down naturally for 15 minutes.
12. Release any leftover pressure.

13. Serve with cilantro, salt, and pepper on top of rice.

<u>Nutritional information (per serving):</u>
Calories - 394
Protein- 31
Carbs - 9
Fat - 26
Fiber - 2

Pork Chops w/ Creamy Mushroom Gravy
Serves: 6
Time: 30 minutes (16 minute cook time)

This tender and rich pork chop recipe is not low-calorie, but it's a great dinner for special occasions like Christmas. The pressure cooker turns the pork chops into mouthwatering cuts, so you never have to eat dry pork again, and the cream of mushroom soup and sour cream melt into a delicious gravy.

<u>Ingredients:</u>
6 pork chops
1 ½ cups sour cream
1 ½ cups water
1 (10.5-ounce) can of cream of mushroom soup
2-3 tablespoons olive oil
1 tablespoon chopped parsley
2 teaspoons chicken bouillon powder
Pepper to taste

Cooking Tip
You can substitute Greek Yogurt for the sour cream, if desired.

<u>Directions:</u>

1. On the "sauté" setting, heat the olive oil.
2. Season the pork chops with pepper.
3. Add to the pressure cooker and brown on both sides, plating as you go.
4. Deglaze the pot with water and chicken bouillon.
5. Put the chops back in the pot.
6. Secure lid and cook on high pressure for 16 minutes.
7. Turn off the cooker and let the pressure drop naturally.
8. Remove the chops.
9. Pour in the soup and heat on the lowest heat setting.
10. Add the sour cream into the cooker and heat through. Be careful since this can easily curdle. Don't let it boil.
11. Quickly stir in the parsley and pour over the pork chops.

Nutritional information (per serving):
Calories - 284.6
Protein- 23.2
Carbs - 10.6
Fat - 16.2
Fiber - 0

Shredded BBQ Pork
Serves: 16
Time: 75 minutes (60-70 minute cook time)

BBQ pork sandwiches are one of the highlights of summer. Tender, spicy 'n sweet, strands of pork with cool coleslaw and fresh corn on the cob...it's hard to beat that. While other BBQ pork recipes take hours and hours, the pressure cooker lets you cook up 16 servings in just over one hour.

Ingredients:
8 pounds pork butt roast

2 (12-ounce) bottles of your favorite BBQ sauce
1 teaspoon garlic powder
Salt and pepper

Directions:
1. Season your pork with garlic, pepper, and salt.
2. Lay in the pressure cooker and fill with enough water so the meat is covered.
3. Secure pressure cooker lid and cook on high pressure for about 1 hour and ten minutes. Pork should be at 145-degrees Fahrenheit to be safe.
4. Quick-release the pressure and drain, leaving about 2 cups of the cooking liquid.
5. Shred the pork with a fork and mix in the BBQ sauce. Use the cooking liquid until you get the desired result.

Nutritional information (per serving):
Calories - 353
Protein- 23.1
Carbs - 15.4
Fat - 21.3
Fiber - .3

Pork Sirloin Tip Roast
Serves: 6-8
Time: 35 minutes (25 minute cook time)

Pork can be hard to cook. You have to make sure it's cooked all the way through, but if it's overcooked, it's dry and unpleasant. The solution is your electric pressure cooker. This recipe combines a nice 3-pound pork sirloin roast with apple juice, chili powder, and other seasonings for a dinner fit for holidays like Christmas and New Year's.

Ingredients:

3 pound pork sirloin tip roast
1 cup water
½ cup apple juice
1 tablespoon vegetable oil
½ teaspoon salt
½ teaspoon black pepper
½ teaspoon garlic powder
½ teaspoon onion powder
¼ teaspoon chili powder

Directions:

1. Mix spices and rub over the pork roast.
2. Heat oil in the pressure cooker on the "browning" setting.
3. When hot, brown the roast on both sides.
4. Pour in the water and apple juice.
5. Secure the lid and cook on high pressure for 25 minutes.
6. When time is up, let the pressure come down naturally for 5 minutes, and then quick-release the rest.
7. Serve with fresh, steamed root veggies, mashed potatoes, or your other favorite side dish.

Nutritional information (per serving):

Calories - 214
Protein- 39
Carbs - 2
Fat - 3
Fiber - 0

Braised Pork w/ Peas and White Beans

Serves: 6-8
Time: 40 minutes (30 minute cook time)

Braised pork in a pressure cooker become melt-in-your-mouth nuggets of goodness you won't believe only cooked for a half hour. Tender white beans, carrots, onions, and a bag of frozen peas serve as your veggies, and just two tablespoons of Italian seasoning brings all the flavors together into a fresh, tasty dish. Since the beans are dried, plan on soaking them for an hour or so before beginning the recipe.

Ingredients:

3 cups chicken broth
2-3 pounds of trimmed boneless pork shoulder cut into 1-inch cubes
2 pounds carrots, cut into 1-inch pieces
16-ounce bag frozen peas
6-8 cloves chopped garlic
2 onions, cut into ½-inch pieces
8 ounces of dried white beans
4 bay leaves
1 cup dry white wine
2 tablespoons Italian seasoning herb mix

Directions:

1. Rinse the beans and cover with hot water with a tablespoon of salt. Let them sit for at least an hour.
2. In a skillet (NOT your pressure cooker), heat a splash of olive oil and sauté the chopped garlic and onions until they begin to brown.
3. Add another dash of oil, this time to the pressure cooker, and brown the pork shoulder.
4. When the onions/garlic are brown, add them to the pressure cooker.
5. Pour the white wine into the skillet where you browned the onions and garlic, and deglaze.

6. Add this liquid to the pressure cooker, along with another cup of white wine.
7. Drain the white beans (do not rinse) and toss in the pressure cooker along with the carrots.
8. Pour in the chicken broth and herb mix.
9. Secure the pressure cooker lid and cook on high pressure for 30 minutes.
10. When the timer goes off, let the pressure come down naturally for 10-15 minutes, and then finish off with a quick-release.
11. Add the bag of frozen peas and mix until they are heated through.
12. Serve with a generous spoonful of the veggies and enjoy!

Nutritional information (per serving):
Calories - 645
Protein- 50
Carbs - 42
Fat - 29
Fiber - 5

Pressure-Cooker Herbed Pork Roast
Serves: 4
Time: 25 minutes (17 minute cook time)

This simple herbed pork roast is a great option for weekdays when you're tired of the usual chicken-or-beef routine. It feels elegant, but only has 11 total ingredients, including fresh and earthy herbs like rosemary and basil. Cubed potatoes help round out the recipe and fill you up.

Ingredients:
1 ½ pounds boneless pork loin

3 peeled, cubed medium potatoes
½ cup chicken stock
1 peeled and crushed garlic clove
1 tablespoon olive oil
1 teaspoon thyme
1 teaspoon crushed rosemary
½ teaspoon marjoram
½ teaspoon basil
Salt and pepper to taste

Directions:
1. Season the pork with salt and pepper.
2. Heat oil in your cooker and brown the potatoes until they have a gold color.
3. Carefully take them out and set aside.
4. Add some more oil if necessary, and brown the pork roast on all sides.
5. Toss in the crushed garlic, wait a few moments, and then add the herbs so they are evenly-distributed on the roast.
6. Pour in the broth.
7. Secure the pressure cooker lid and cook on high pressure for 17 minutes.
8. When time is up, quick-release the pressure and test the meat with a meat thermometer. It should read at least 145-degrees Fahrenheit.
9. Add the potatoes and cook again on high pressure for 5 more minutes.
10. Quick-release and serve!

Nutritional information (1 slice per serving):
Calories - 145
Protein- 24
Carbs - 0

Fat - 5
Fiber - 0

Kalua Pig in a Pressure Cooker

Serves: 8
Time: 1 hour, 45 minutes (100 minute cook time)

If you love shredded pork, but want something different than the usual BBQ pork sandwich, try this Hawaiian version. The meat and cabbage become incredibly tender and there's even bacon involved, so you know it's going to be good. You stick the garlic cloves right into the roast, so the meat becomes infused with delicious flavor.

Ingredients:
5 pound bone-in pork shoulder roast
5 peeled garlic cloves
3 slices of bacon
1 cup water
1 cored cabbage, cut into 6 wedges
1 ½ tablespoons coarse Hawaiian red sea salt

> **Cooking Tip**
> If you can't find Hawaiian sea salt, coarse rock salt or Kosher salt is okay, too. Just look for salt that's unrefined.

Directions:
1. Sauté the bacon in your pressure cooker. When it is nice and brown on both sides, turn off the heat.
2. While that cooks, cut the pork roast into three equally-sized pieces.

3. Make a few slits in the pork and stick in the whole, peeled garlic cloves.
4. Rub the pork pieces with salt and lay on top of the bacon in a single layer.
5. Pour in 1 cup of water or whatever the minimum liquid requirement is for your electric pressure cooker.
6. Secure the lid and cook on high pressure for 90 minutes.
7. When time is up, turn off the cooker and let the pressure come down on its own.
8. Remove the meat.
9. If the cooking liquid is too salty, add more water before putting in the six cabbage wedges.
10. Close lid and cook again on high pressure for 3-5 minutes.
11. Quick-release the pressure.
12. In the meantime, shred the pork.
13. When the cabbage is done, plate, and top with the shredded pork.

Nutritional information (5-oz per serving):
Calories - 415
Protein- 30
Carbs - 5
Fat - 30
Fiber - 2

Chicken

Balsamic Chicken Breasts and Pearl Onions
Serves: 6-7
Time: 22 minutes (17 minute cook time)

This chicken breast recipe has it all: sweetness, saltiness, creaminess, and some crunch. It gets its rich, sophisticated flavors from red wine and balsamic vinegar. The ingredients are also pretty easy to get, and you can get fresh or frozen veggies if you need to.

Ingredients:
2 pounds chicken breasts
4 garlic cloves
1 ham hock
2 cups pearl onions
2 cups chopped carrots
2 bay leaves
1 cup golden raisins
½ cup chicken broth
¼ cup balsamic vinegar
¼ cup red wine vinegar

Directions:
1. Season both sides of the chicken breasts with salt and pepper.
2. In the pressure cooker, put the chicken and ham hock at the bottom, and then add everything else.
3. Secure the pressure cooker lid.
4. Select the "poultry" or "chicken" setting. You can also program it for high pressure for 17 minutes.
5. When the timer goes off, quick-release the pressure.
6. Remove the chicken from the pressure cooker and set aside.
7. Pour out half of the liquid (don't throw away!) and whisk in some cornstarch to thicken it.
8. Return the liquid to the pressure cooker and simmer.
9. Once the sauce has thickened to your liking, return the chicken to the pot.

10. Serve right away, or keep the pressure cooker on the "keep warm" setting until you're ready.

Nutritional information (per serving):
Calories - 281
Protein- 30
Carbs - 27
Fat - 6
Fiber - 1

Hawaiian BBQ Chicken
Serves: 7-8
Time: 15 minutes (10 minute cook time)

If you love the flavors of BBQ, but don't have a grill, a pressure cooker is the next best thing. This BBQ chicken recipe takes a tropical detour with the pineapple and coconut milk, so you get sweetness in addition to the heat from chili flakes and the BBQ sauce. Unlike most good barbeque which takes hours, this recipe only takes about 15 minutes.

Ingredients:
3 pounds chicken breasts
2 cups diced pineapples
1 cup BBQ sauce (your choice)
1 cup coconut milk
1 teaspoon chili flakes

Directions:
1. Begin by mixing the coconut milk, BBQ sauce, and chili flakes.
2. In the bottom of your pressure cooker, lay down the pineapples.

3. Dip the pieces of chicken in the BBQ sauce and lay them in the pot.
4. Pour over the rest of the sauce.
5. Secure the pressure cooker lid and set the timer for 10 minutes.
6. When time is up, quick-release the pressure.
7. Take out the chicken with tongs and plate.
8. Turn on the "browning" program and reduce the sauce mixture so it begins to thick.
9. When the sauce is ready, add the chicken back in.
10. Serve with rice and a squirt of lime juice.

Nutritional information (per serving):
Calories -353
Protein- 46.3
Carbs - 23.9
Fat - 6
Fiber - .6

Curried Chicken and Spinach
Serves: 5-6
Time: 6 minutes (4 minute cook time)

If you're tired of your old chicken recipes, this is a great one to try. It combines tender chicken with spinach in a tasty tomato-based curry sauce. You can eat as is or like a spaghetti sauce with noodles, though keep in mind this will add more calories.

Ingredients:
2 ½ pounds boneless chicken, cut into 1-inch pieces
1 ½ cups chunky tomato sauce
½ cup chicken broth
2 (10-ounce packages) frozen spinach
1 tablespoon mild curry powder

Chopped cilantro

1. Pour the chicken broth in the pressure cooker and add chicken.
2. Layer the frozen on top and pour on the sauce.
3. Add the curry powder and stir into the sauce. Do NOT stir the sauce with the chicken.
4. Secure the pressure cooker lid and cook on high pressure for 4 minutes.
5. When time is up, quick-release the pressure.
6. Stir everything together and season if necessary.
7. Serve with the chopped cilantro strewn on top.

Nutritional information (per 100g serving):
Calories - 282
Protein- 6.7
Carbs - 3.5
Fat - 26.8
Fiber - .8

Chicken Prosciutto Rolls
Serves: 6
Time: 15 minutes (10 minute cook time)

Delicate chicken breasts are pounded into thin cutlets and rolled with salty prosciutto for a delicious, quick-cooking dinner. This recipe is served with peas and seasoned with sage, bringing you the fresh, deep flavors of Italy in only 10 minutes. You can make the meal more complete and serve with a side like creamy polenta or mashed potatoes.

Ingredients:
6 chicken breasts

6 slices of prosciutto

10 sage leaves

1 cup frozen peas

¾ cup chicken broth

¼ cup white wine

1 tablespoon olive oil

1 tablespoon butter

1 teaspoon salt

Directions:

1. Prepare the chicken for rolling by covering with a piece of wax paper and pounding with a mallet.
2. Layer each breast with a slice of prosciutto and rolling tightly. Pin with a toothpick, along with a sage leaf.
3. In your electric pressure cooker, heat the butter, oil, and other sage leaves on "sauté."
4. Turn to the "browning" setting and lay down the rolls leaf-side down to brown. Brown on both sides.
5. When they're ready, turn over the leaf-side that is facing up, and pour over the white wine.
6. Let the wine cook off before adding your stock and salt.
7. Pour the frozen peas on top and secure the pressure cooker lid.
8. Cook on high pressure for 5-7 minutes.
9. Quick-release the pressure.
10. Serve the rolls with the peas and a ladle of the cooking liquid.

Nutritional information (per serving):

Calories -308

Protein- 35

Carbs - 3

Fat - 13

Fiber - 1

Pressure-Cooker Chicken Gumbo

Serves: 6-8
Time: 1 hour (10 minute cook time)

This hearty New Orleans staple is perfect for long, cold winter nights. It makes great leftovers as well, so even if you don't have 8 people in your family, go ahead and make it in your 6-quart pressure cooker. The gumbo is bursting with flavors from the smoked sausage, Cajun spice rub, and veggies like onion, bell pepper, and tomatoes.

Ingredients:
2 quarts chicken stock
1 pound andouille sausage, 1-inch thick pieces
1 pound boneless, skinless chicken thighs, 2-inch pieces
4 crushed garlic cloves
1 minced onion
1 minced celery stalk
1 minced bell pepper
1 (15-ounce) can diced tomatoes
½ cup flour
¼ cup veggie oil
1 tablespoon veggie oil
1 teaspoon salt
1 teaspoon Cajun spice rub
Salt and pepper to taste
Tabasco to taste
Parsley

Directions:
1. Heat 1 tablespoon of the oil in your pressure cooker.
2. Add the sausage and turn the cooker to the "browning" setting and brown on both sides.

3. Take out the sausage with a slotted spoon, so most of the oil stays in the pot.
4. Add the chicken and brown on both sides.
5. Take out the chicken (leaving fat and oil in the cooker) and put with the sausage.
6. Next, you will make the roux. Mix ¼ cup veggie oil, Cajun spice, and flour to the pressure cooker. Stir uncovered until the mixture becomes smooth and tan.
7. Add the celery, garlic, bell pepper, and onion to the pot. Sprinkle with salt and stir for about 5 minutes until they become soft.
8. Add the chicken and sausage back to the pressure cooker. Pour in the chicken broth and deglaze the pot.
9. Add the can of diced tomatoes.
10. Secure the pressure cooker and cook on high pressure for 10 minutes.
11. When the timer beeps, turn off the cooker and let the pressure decrease on its own.
12. Carefully remove the lid and season if necessary with salt, pepper, and some Tabasco.
13. Serve over white rice or as is! Sprinkle some chopped parsley on top.

Nutritional information (per serving, just the gumbo):
Calories - 521
Protein- 27.8
Carbs - 26.3
Fat - 32.5
Fiber - 2.4

Whole Chicken in a Pressure Cooker
Serves: 10
Time: 45 minutes (35 minute cook time)

Cooking a whole chicken may seem intimidating if you've never tried before. However, it is a great way to cook chicken to use in a variety of meals, and to get a chicken carcass to make chicken broth. An electric pressure cooker is the easiest method, and the whole process takes less than an hour.

<u>Ingredients:</u>
1 4-pound organic chicken
6 peeled garlic cloves
1 ½ cups chicken broth
2 tablespoon lemon juice
1 tablespoon coconut oil
1 teaspoon paprika
1 teaspoon dried thyme
½ teaspoon salt
¼ teaspoon black pepper

<u>Directions:</u>
1. Mix salt, thyme, pepper, and paprika in a bowl.
2. Rub this seasoning mix on the chicken.
3. In your pressure cooker, heat the oil on the "sauté" setting.
4. Add your chicken so the breast is lying down. Cook for 6-7 minutes.
5. Turn the bird over and add the garlic, lemon juice, and broth.
6. Secure the pressure cooker lid and cook on high pressure for 25 minutes.
7. When time is up, turn off the cooker and let the pressure come down naturally.
8. Carefully remove the chicken from the cooker and let it rest for about 5 minutes before cutting into it.

<u>Nutritional information (per serving):</u>

Calories - 413
Protein- 28
Carbs - .8
Fat - 30
Fiber - .1

Pesto Chicken w/ Carrots + New Potatoes

Serves: 4
Time: 20 minutes (11 minute cook time)

This recipe uses budget-friendly chicken thighs and jarred pesto to create a tasty and nutritious meal for a family of four. It's a great meal for any season, and for those busy work nights when you don't want to spend a lot of time in the kitchen. After browning the meat, just throw everything into a pressure cooker and you're good to go!

Ingredients:
3 pounds chicken thighs (bone-in, no skin, trimmed)
8 new red potatoes
1 large peeled onion, cut into ½ slices
1 pound baby carrots
½ cup chicken broth
⅓cup pesto
½ teaspoon olive oil

Directions:
1. Toss the chicken in the olive oil and brown in the pressure cooker once it's been preheated. About four thighs will fit in 6-quart cooker.
2. After three minutes on each side (six minutes total), take out the chicken and coat in the pesto. Repeat with the remaining chicken.

3. Pour in stock and onions and place the steamer rack inside the pressure cooker.
4. Add the chicken on the rack and top with carrots and potatoes.
5. Secure the lid and cook on high pressure for 11 minutes.
6. Quick-release the pressure.
7. Serve right away and enjoy!

Nutritional information (per serving):
Calories - 467
Protein- 47
Carbs - 19
Fat - 6
Fiber - 6

Teriyaki Chicken Bowls

Serves: 4
Time: 30 minutes (20 minute cook time)

Take-out Chinese food used to be one of my guilty pleasures, but the amount of sodium and MSG started to make me sick every time I got it. If you love the flavors of Chinese, but don't want all the additives, this teriyaki chicken prepared in the pressure cooker is a great recipe for when you get a craving.

Ingredients:
2 pounds boneless, skinless chicken thighs
½ cup water
½ cup low-sodium soy sauce
2 minced garlic cloves
2 tablespoons rice vinegar
2 tablespoons honey
2 tablespoons brown sugar
1 tablespoon cornstarch

1 tablespoon grated ginger
2 tablespoons water
1 teaspoon hot sauce
Chopped scallions
Roasted peanuts

Directions:
1. In your pressure cooker, whisk the water, rice vinegar, honey, brown sugar, ginger, garlic, hot sauce, and soy sauce together.
2. Add the chicken thighs and stir to coat.
3. Secure the lid and cook on high pressure for 20 minutes.
4. Quick-release the pressure.
5. In a separate bowl, mix the cornstarch and water.

Cooking Tip
When you mix cornstarch and water together, they will dissolve together faster if the water is very cold. If cornstarch comes into contact with a too-warm liquid, it can clump up.

6. Add to the cooker to thicken. Cook for a few minutes on the sauté mode to get everything simmering.
7. Serve with brown rice and garnished with scallions and roasted peanuts.

Nutritional information (per serving):
Calories - 520
Protein- 52
Carbs - 46
Fat - 14

Coconut Chicken Curry

Serves: 6
Time: 40 minutes (30 minute cook time)

This sweet and spicy chicken curry comes together surprisingly quickly. It may look a bit scary because of all the ingredients, but you can sub the whole spices (cloves, cardamom pods, etc.) with garam masala powder if you want.

Ingredients:
2 ½ - 3 pounds of boneless, skinless chicken thighs
2 sliced yellow onions
2 sliced tomatoes
2 minced garlic cloves
1 tablespoon vinegar
1 tablespoon coconut oil
1-inch piece of peeled and minced ginger
3 teaspoons salt

For the spice paste:
6 peeled and halved shallots
4 whole cloves
4 dried red chilies
3 green cardamom pods
1-inch cinnamon stick
¾ cup grated, unsweetened coconut
2 teaspoons coriander seeds
2 teaspoons black peppercorns
2 teaspoons fennel seeds
1 teaspoon turmeric powder
1 teaspoon cumin seeds
1 teaspoon black mustard seeds

Directions:

1. Begin by making the curry paste. Heat the electric pressure cooker on its "Sauté" setting.
2. Toss in the shallots and red chilies until black spots appear.
3. Remove from the cooker and set aside for later.
4. Cook the coconut and whole spices (not the powder) in the pressure cooker until they are fragrant and the coconut has browned a little. If you are using just the garam masala, cook the coconut first and then mix in the powder with the turmeric.
5. Move the coconut and spices to a food processor along with the red chilies.
6. Blend until smooth along with 4-6 tablespoons of water. You should end up with a creamy paste.
7. For the chicken, begin by adding oil to the cooker.
8. When the oil is hot, add the garlic, onions, and ginger.
9. Sauté for 10-15 minutes until the onions are soft.
10. Add your creamy paste and cook for 1 minute.
11. Next, add the tomatoes and fry again for 5 more minutes until the tomatoes have cooked down.
12. Add your chicken, vinegar, and salt and mix.
13. Secure the cooker lid and cook on high pressure for 10 minutes.
14. Let the pressure come down naturally.
15. If the chicken isn't done yet, cook for another four minutes, and then quick-release.
16. Serve on a bed of basmati rice.

Nutritional information (per serving):

Calories - 444
Protein- 45
Carbs - 25

Fat - 18.5
Fiber - 7.1

Lemon-Olive Ligurian Chicken

Serves: 6-8

Time: 20 minutes (10 minute cook time, *2-4 hours marinate time*)

This fresh, brightly-flavored chicken recipe comes from northwest Italy, where olives and lemon are aplenty. It makes a great, low-calorie summertime meal that's also low in carbs and high in protein. When planning this dish, keep in mind you want to marinate the raw chicken for 2-4 hours to really get that full flavor. In terms of putting it all together, the electric pressure cooker speeds up the process.

Ingredients:
1 package bone-in chicken pieces
3.5 ounces of Kalamata olives
½ cup dry white wine
4 tablespoons extra virgin olive oil
½ bunch parsley leaves w/ stems
3 juiced lemons
3 sprigs fresh rosemary
2 chopped garlic cloves
2 sprigs fresh sage
1 teaspoon salt
¼ teaspoon pepper

Directions:
1. To make the marinade, chop the rosemary, sage, parsley, and garlic together.
2. Add lemon juice, salt, pepper, and olive oil, and stir.
3. Cover the raw chicken with the marinade and wrap.

4. Store in the fridge for 2-4 hours.
5. When you're ready to make the chicken, begin by heating olive oil in the pressure cooker.
6. Brown the chicken pieces for 5 minutes and plate.
7. Deglaze the pot with the white wine until it evaporates.
8. Put the chicken back in, dark meat first.
9. Pour the rest of the marinade in. If the pressure cooker is 8-quarts and up, pour in ½ cup of water.
10. Secure the pressure cooker lid and cook on high pressure for 10 minutes.
11. Quick-release the pressure and carefully remove the chicken.
12. Continue simmering the cooking liquid uncovered until it becomes thick.
13. Put the chicken back in just to warm it up and simmer in the sauce.
14. Serve with lemon slices, olives, and fresh rosemary.

Nutritional information (per serving):
Calories - 204.8
Protein- 17.8
Carbs - 3.1
Fat - 12.2
Fiber - .3

Easy Buffalo Chicken Wings
Serves: 4-6
Time: 30 minutes (25 minute cook time)

Buffalo wings are a bar classic, and even more delicious when you make them at home. The tangy-and-sweet coating of hot sauce and honey satisfies every craving, and the dipping sauce is made out of whole-milk yogurt and parsley instead of bleu cheese dressing for fewer calories.

Ingredients:
24 chicken wings
4 tablespoons hot sauce
¼ cup tomato puree
¼ cup honey
3 teaspoons salt
1 cup whole-milk, plain yogurt
1 tablespoon parsley

Directions:
1. Pour one cup of water into your pressure cooker and add the wings to the steamer basket. Do not crowd them.
2. Secure the pressure cooker lid and cook for 10 minutes on high pressure.
3. In a separate bowl, combine the tomato puree, hot sauce, honey, and salt until the honey dissolves.
4. When the timer goes off, quick-release the pressure.
5. Remove the wings and coat in the sauce.
6. Arrange them on a baking sheet lined with parchment paper and stick under the broiler for 5 minutes.
7. Serve with celery sticks and whole-milk yogurt mixed with a tablespoon of parsley.

Nutritional information (per serving):
Calories - 436
Protein- 25
Carbs - 15
Fat - 24
Fiber - 0

Spicy Cornish Game Hen
Serves: 2

Time: 30 minutes (25 minute cook time)

If you're looking for something a little different than chicken for a romantic dinner for two, this is a fantastic recipe. You get two servings from just one hen, which is flavored with hot sauce, Worcestershire, and just a bit of garlic and onions.

Ingredients:
1 cornish game hen
4 celery ribs
2 cups baby carrots
1 cup water
⅓ cup chopped green onions
2 tablespoons chopped garlic
2 tablespoons olive oil
2 tablespoons chopped onion
1 tablespoon Worcestershire sauce
2 teaspoons hot sauce
Salt and pepper to taste

Directions:
1. Heat olive oil in the pressure cooker on the "sauté" or "browning" setting.
2. Place the hen in the cooker and brown for 3 minutes on each side.
3. Mix all the other ingredients (except the green onion) in a bowl and pour into the cooker.
4. Secure the lid and cook on high pressure for 15 minutes.
5. Let the pressure come down by itself before opening.
6. Serve with a garnish of green onions and seasonings to taste.

Nutritional information (per serving):
Calories - 336

Protein- 26
Carbs - 18.4
Fat - 17.9
Fiber - 3.9

Cranberry Turkey Wings
Serves: 4
Time: 40 minutes (30 minute cook time)

In case you were worried, I know that turkey is not a type of chicken. However, this poultry recipe is too good not to share, so here we are. It's a great way to use turkey besides just baking or frying it, and the cranberries add an addicting tangy sweetness to the tender meat.

Ingredients:
4 turkey wings
1 ½ cups fresh cranberries
1 sliced onion
1 cup shelled walnuts
1 cup orange juice w/ no added sugar
1 bunch fresh thyme
2 tablespoons oil
2 tablespoons butter

Directions:
1. Preheat your electric cooker for a few minutes.
2. When it's warm, add the oil and butter and melt.
3. Brown the turkey wings on both sides and season with salt and pepper.
4. Take out the turkey legs to add the onions, and then put the turkey legs back in the cooker, so they are on top of the onion.
5. Add the cranberries, thyme, and walnuts.

6. Pour the orange juice over the meat.
7. Secure the pressure cooker lid and cook on high pressure for 25 minutes.
8. When the timer beeps, turn off the cooker and wait 10 minutes.
9. If the pressure is not all gone, quick-release the rest.
10. Pick out the thyme.
11. Carefully move the turkey to a dish and broil for 5 minutes.
12. Meanwhile, simmer the liquid in the cooker until it is reduced by half.
13. Pour this sauce over the turkeys before serving.

Nutritional information (1 wing per serving):
Calories - 340
Protein- 6
Carbs - 16
Fat -19
Fiber - 0

Braised Quill w/ a Carrot + Fennel Nest

Serves: 2
Time: 25 minutes (20 minute cook time)

Here's another non-chicken poultry recipe coming your way! This is a very sophisticated dish that is bound to impress your significant other or a lucky friend. The quail is stuffed with some thyme and rosemary, and braised with sparkling white wine, smoky pancetta, and scallions. The birds are then served on a "nest" of carrots and fennel matchsticks for a beautiful plating.

Ingredients:
2 cleaned, emptied, and rinsed quails

4 big, thick thinly-chopped carrots
3.5-ounces of diced smoked pancetta
2 chopped scallions
½ cup sparkling white wine
1 bunch of rosemary
1 bunch of thyme
1 bay leaf
½ thinly- chopped fennel chop
1 lemon
Rocket arugula
Salt and pepper to taste

Directions:
1. Use a mandolin to cut the carrots and fennel into very thin sticks.
2. Put the steamer basket with the veggies into the cooker with the minimum amount of water required.
3. Secure the lid and cook for 1 minute on high.
4. Quick-release the pressure.
5. Quickly, remove the steamer basket and run cold water over the veggies.
6. Save the steaming liquid.
7. In the now-empty cooker, add the shallots, rosemary, thyme, pancetta, bay leaf, and a swirl of oil. Save a few bunches of the rosemary and thyme.
8. Season and begin to sauté.
9. Stuff the quails with the remaining bunches of rosemary and thyme.
10. When the shallots are soft, move the pressure cooker contents to the side and put the quails down, breast facing down.
11. Brown on all sides before turning so the breast is pointing up.
12. Pour in the white wine and deglaze.

13. Simmer for 3 minutes until ⅓ of the wine is left.
14. Pour in the saved steaming liquid and close the pressure cooker.
15. Cook on high pressure for 10 minutes
16. Quick-release the pressure when time is up.
17. Move the quails to a plate.
18. Pull out as much of the herbs as you can from the quails' cavity.
19. Strain the cooking liquid and return to the cooker to reduce.
20. Build a "nest" with the fennel, carrots, and arugula.
21. Season with olive oil and a squirt of lemon juice.
22. Return the quails to the reduced cooking liquid and coat.
23. After about 2 minutes, the quails will be warmed up and ready to serve.

Nutritional information (1 quail + nest per serving):
Calories - 402
Protein- 32
Carbs - 20
Fat -10
Fiber - 1

Homemade Chicken Stock
Makes: 3 quarts
Time: 1 hour, 10 minutes (50 minute cook time)

Homemade stock can be made quickly and is more nutritious than the store-bought version. It is also an easy way to improve your soups and stews, especially if you feel that cooking everything quickly in a pressure cooker results in less flavor than if you slowly simmer.

Ingredients:

12 cups water
3 pounds chicken parts, bones included
2 smashed garlic cloves
1 yellow onion, cut into quarters with the peel on
1 scrubbed carrot, cut into 3-inch pieces
2 tablespoons lemon juice
2 bay leaves
1 tablespoon olive oil
Salt and pepper to taste

Directions:

1. Begin by browning the chicken. Heat the oil in your pressure cooker and lay the chicken down in a single layer.
2. When brown on both sides, remove and replace with onions to brown.
3. Deglaze the pot with a few cups of water before adding the chicken, carrots, lemon juice, garlic, salt, pepper, and bay leaves.
4. Pour in the rest of the water.
5. Secure the lid and cook on high pressure for 50 minutes.
6. When the timer beeps, turn off the cooker and let the pressure come down by itself.
7. When depressurized, open the cooker and strain the broth through a cheesecloth-lined sieve.
8. Throw out the solids.
9. Cool the stock and then store in the fridge or freeze.

Nutritional information (per serving):

Calories - 31
Protein- 2.6
Carbs - .2

Fat - 2.2
Fiber - 0

Beef

Easy Homemade Meat Sauce
Serves: 3-4
Time: 12 minutes (5 minute cook time)

Meat sauce is something you probably use all the time, but may have never made from scratch. Store-bought sauce is often packed with sugar, so when you make it yourself, you know you're only using the necessary amount. You'll also know the sauce doesn't have artificial ingredients, and you'll probably save a lot of money because you don't have to buy organic jarred sauce. You can make this sauce along with the pasta, if you want, or you can just make the sauce and store it for later use.

Ingredients;
1 pound ground beef
1 ½ cups water
1 ½ cups chopped onion
½ cup dry red wine
¼ cup chopped fresh parsley
¼ cup grated parmesan
28-ounces crushed tomatoes
2 tablespoons olive oil
1 teaspoon whole fennel seeds
1 teaspoon garlic powder
¾ teaspoon salt
¼ teaspoon crushed red pepper flakes

Directions:

1. Heat 1 tablespoon of oil in your pressure cooker.
2. Brown the ground meat and stir until it's all broken up.
3. Add the fennel seeds and onions and cook for another 1-2 minutes.
4. Deglaze the pot with the wine and bring to a boil.
5. When about 1 minute has passed, add the salt, garlic, and water. Bring to a boil again.
6. If you're cooking the pasta with the sauce, add now, along with the tomatoes on top.
7. Do not stir before closing the pressure cooker lid.
8. Cook on high pressure for 5 minutes.
9. Quick-release the pressure.
10. Add the cheese, parsley, another tablespoon of oil, and crushed red pepper flakes.
11. Stir well.
12. Let the sauce sit for 3-5 minutes. If you're cooking the pasta, and it isn't tender yet, turn on the "sauté" setting again and stir until it meets your standards.

Nutritional information (1 cup per serving, just the sauce):
Calories - 281
Protein- 16.28
Carbs - 21
Fat -16
Fiber - 4.5

Beef-Stuffed Cabbage

Serves: 4
Time: 50 minutes (40 minute cook time)

This Hungarian-style stuffed cabbage combines chopped beef with tender cabbage, rice, and sauerkraut. It is a hearty meal and will definitely fill you up during cold autumn or winter days.

Ingredients:

1 pound chopped beef
1 head cabbage leaves
1 cup water
1 cup tomato sauce
8 ounces of rinsed and drained sauerkraut
1 chopped onion
¼ cup rice
2 tablespoons chicken stock
1 tablespoon minced parsley
Sour cream/yogurt
Salt and pepper to taste

Directions:
1. Pour the water into the cooker so it's filled halfway, and boil.
2. Add several leaves and cook till softened.
3. Drain the leaves and set aside.
4. Dry out the pressure cooker with a paper towel (once it's cooled), and pour in the 1 cup of water, tomato sauce, salt, pepper, and sauerkraut.
5. Mix.
6. In a separate bowl, mix the onion, meat, parsley, rice, and chicken stock.
7. Season.
8. Put 2 tablespoons of the meat filling into each cabbage leaf, fold the sides, and then roll.
9. Put these rolls in the cooker on top of the sauerkraut/tomato sauce mixture.
10. Secure the lid and cook on high pressure for 40 minutes.

11. Wait until the pressure decreases naturally before opening the lid.
12. Serve with sour cream or yogurt.

Nutritional information (1 roll per serving):
Calories - 117
Protein- 8.81
Carbs - 8.97
Fat -5.3
Fiber - 1.2

Beef 'n Broccoli
Serves: 6
Time: 18 minutes (12 minute cook time)

Tender beef strips and broccoli florets are cooked in rich beef broth, onion, soy sauce, and sugar for a homemade take on the Asian restaurant classic. This recipe is especially good for busy weeknights when you don't have much time to cook, but want a healthy alternative to drive-thru fast food.

Ingredients:
1 ½ pounds trimmed, sliced boneless beef chuck roast
4 minced garlic cloves
1 pound broccoli florets
1 chopped onion
¾ cup beef broth
½ cup soy sauce
⅓cup brown sugar
3 tablespoons cornstarch
3 tablespoons water
2 tablespoons sesame oil
2 teaspoons olive oil
⅛ teaspoon red pepper flakes

Salt and pepper to taste

Directions:
1. Begin by seasoning your beef with pepper and salt.
2. Heat olive oil in your pressure cooker on the "browning" setting.
3. When it's hot, add the meat in batches and brown on both sides.
4. Move meat to a plate.
5. Choose "sauté" and soften the onion.
6. Once soft, add the garlic and sauté for another minute.
7. Pour in the broth, brown sugar, sesame oil, soy sauce, and red pepper flakes and stir until the sugar dissolves.
8. Put the beef back in and cook on high pressure for 12 minutes.
9. Meanwhile, microwave the broccoli with ¼ cup of water for 3-4 minutes until the broccoli is softened.
10. Quick-release the pressure cooker.
11. In a bowl, mix the cornstarch and water. Pour into the pressure cooker.
12. Bring to a boil on the "browning" setting to thicken.
13. Add the broccoli.
14. Serve with rice and enjoy!

Nutritional information (per serving):
Calories - 344
Protein- 26.5
Carbs - 15.9
Fat -21.5
Fiber - 7.4

From-Scratch Sloppy Joe's
Serves: 7-8
Time: 15 minutes (10 minute cook time)

Kids love Sloppy Joe's. Juicy hamburger meat becomes sweet thanks to classic ingredients like ketchup, Worcestershire, and sugar, and you can add other seasonings like red pepper flakes if you want a bit more spice. Instead of simmering for nearly a half-hour to really get that full flavor, a pressure cooker can get the job done from start to finish in 15 minutes.

Ingredients:
2 pounds ground beef
¾ cup ketchup
1 chopped onion
¼ cup chopped green pepper (optional)
2 tablespoons Worcestershire sauce
2 tablespoons mustard
1 tablespoon sugar
2 teaspoons steak seasoning
1 teaspoon garlic

Directions:
1. Heat a splash of olive oil in your electric pressure cooker.
2. When hot, brown the hamburger meat.
3. When the meat is ready, throw in all the other ingredients and stir well.
4. Secure the lid and cook on high pressure for 10 minutes.
5. Serve on hamburger buns as is or with optional toppings like pickles, cheese, and so on.

Nutritional information (per serving w/ bun):
Calories - 300
Protein- 28.3
Carbs - 32

Fat -21.5
Fiber - 1

Classic Beef Pot Roast w/ Gravy

Serves: 12
Time: 50 minutes (40 minute cook time)

Nothing soothes the soul quite like some classic comfort food. This classic beef pot roast serves up enough servings for 12 people, making it a great option for a one-pot, big family dinners during the holidays. It comes with its own gravy and veggies, too, including parsnips, carrots, onion, and beautiful Yukon gold potatoes.

Ingredients:
3 pounds trimmed, boneless chuck roast
3 cups beef stock (homemade, ideally)
1 pound turnips, each cut into 8 pieces
1 pound peeled Yukon gold potatoes, cut into 2-inch pieces
3 big, peeled parsnips cut into 2-inch pieces
3 big, peeled carrots cut into 2-inch pieces
1 onion cut into 8 wedges
3 chopped garlic cloves
½ cup dry red wine
4 thyme sprigs tied with twine
2 tablespoons flour
2 teaspoons olive oil
1 teaspoon salt
¼ teaspoon black pepper

Directions:
1. Heat the olive oil in your pressure cooker.
2. While that gets hot, season the roast with salt and pepper.

3. On "brown," cook for about 5 minutes until the roast is browned all over.
4. Add the broth and red wine.
5. Secure the lid and cook on high pressure for 40 minutes.
6. Quick-release the pressure.
7. Add the sprigs, garlic, and veggies.
8. Close the lid again and cook on high pressure for 1 minute.
9. Quick-release and let the cooker stand uncovered for 5 minutes.
10. Carefully take out the roast and vegetables.
11. Cut the roast into thin slices and cover.
12. Now to make the gravy. Strain the liquid from the pressure cooker through a sieve lined with cheesecloth.
13. Throw out any solids.
14. In a skillet, bring the liquid to a boil and cook until it has reduced to about 1 ½ cups.
15. Take out ¼ cup of the liquid and stir in flour with a whisk.
16. Pour this mixture back into the pan and thicken for 2 minutes. Keep stirring with your whisk.
17. Pour gravy over the roast and serve!

Nutritional information (per serving):
Calories - 264
Protein- 23.1
Carbs - 15.4
Fat -11.2
Fiber - 2.6

Homemade Beef Bone Stock
Serves: 10-12

Time: 75 minutes (30 minutes roasting, 34 minutes in pressure cooker)

We already went over how to make homemade chicken stock in the "Chicken" section, but sometimes recipes call for something a bit richer. In its homemade form, beef stock is extremely nutritious because it uses the marrow bones, which are packed with vitamins that help with joint health, digestion, and detoxing. You can drink a cupful of this broth in the mornings for a healthy jumpstart to the day, and use it as a base for countless soups and stews.

Ingredients:
3 pounds beef marrow bones
2 ½ pounds beef shanks, 1-inch thick
8 cups cold water
2 celery stalks cut into 2-inch pieces
1 big, peeled carrot, cut into 2-inch pieces
1 big, peeled onion, cut into 8 pieces
2 bay leaves
½ bunch fresh parsley
2 tablespoons tomato paste
1 tablespoon black peppercorns

Directions:
1. Begin by roasting the meat, bones, and veggies in the oven at 500-degrees.
2. Brush the tomato paste on the bones and shanks, and add to a roasting pan with the onion, celery, and carrots.
3. Roast for 30 minutes.
4. Move all this to your pressure cooker (minimum 6-quarts) and throw in the parsley, bay leaves, and peppercorns.

5. Pour in 8 cups of cold water.
6. Close the pressure cooker lid and cook on high pressure for 35 minutes.
7. Quick-release the pressure and let stand uncovered for 20 minutes.
8. Strain the liquid through a sieve lined with cheesecloth.
9. Get rid of any solids.
10. Pour the broth into a large bowl and chill overnight.
11. Remove any of the solidified fat.
12. This broth will last for 1 week in the fridge or freeze for 3 months.

Nutritional information (per serving):
Calories - 4
Protein- .3
Carbs - .3
Fat -.1
Fiber - .1

Ropa Viejo Pulled Beef

Serves: 6-12
Time: 2 hours, 30 minutes (2 hour cook time)

This Cuban beef dish literally translates into "old clothes," which isn't super appealing, but the recipe itself turns flank steak and veggies into a delicious, stewed wonder that goes great over rice or mashed potatoes. With this recipe, you use both an electric pressure cooker and a stovetop skillet.

Ingredients:
Water
3-3 ½ pounds beef flank steak
4 big ripe tomatoes
2 cups celery

2 big chopped onions
3 bay leaves
3 minced garlic cloves
3 chopped mild chili peppers
1 medium carrot, halved
1 chopped yellow bell pepper
1 cup small green peas
8 tablespoons olive oil
½ cup drained and chopped pimento
1 tablespoon ground cayenne pepper
2 tablespoons tomato paste
1 teaspoon chopped cilantro
½ teaspoon ground cumin
Salt and pepper

Directions:
1. Trim any excess fat from the meat.
2. In a skillet, heat 3 tablespoons of olive oil and brown the meat.
3. Put the meat in the pressure cooker and cover with enough water so the meat is submerged.
4. Add 1 chopped onion to the skillet and soften.
5. Add that to the pressure cooker, along with the carrots and celery.
6. Finish off with the bay leaves.
7. Secure the pressure cooker lid and cook on high pressure for 90 minutes.
8. When the timer goes off, keep on the "Warm" setting.
9. In the skillet from before, heat the rest of the olive and soften the second onion.
10. Add cilantro, garlic, bell pepper, and the peas and simmer for 7 minutes.
11. Add the pimento, tomatoes, chilies, and 2 tablespoons of the tomato paste.

12. Scoop two cups of the cooking liquid from the pressure cooker and pour into the skillet.
13. Add the cayenne pepper, salt, pepper, and cumin to the skillet and stir.
14. Cover the skillet and simmer for 15-20 minutes.
15. Take out the meat and pull apart in a bowl. Pick out the bay leaves.
16. Before you're ready to serve, uncover the skillet and turn the heat up so the gravy thickens a little.
17. Pour over the beef and toss with tongs to get it all blended.
18. Serve with rice, mashed potatoes, polenta, or another side dish of your choice.

Nutritional information (per serving, no side dishes):
Calories - 472
Protein- 40
Carbs - 20
Fat -25.5
Fiber - 4.7

Porcupine Meatballs

Serves: 4-5
Time: 15 minutes (5 minute cook time)

These beef meatballs get their name from the white rice that sticks out from the meat, like porcupine quills. They make a great snack or appetizer, and make their own sauce that you thicken at the very end of the cooking process with a little cornstarch.

Ingredients:
1 ½ pounds ground beef
3 cups tomato sauce

1 cup water
½ cup chopped onion
½ cup uncooked long-grain white rice
¼ chopped parsley
1 minced garlic clove
1 tablespoon cornstarch
½ teaspoon of salt

Directions:
1. Mix all the ingredients (except the water and tomato sauce) to make 17-18 meatballs.
2. Pour the water into your pressure cooker in a single layer. If you still have meatballs left, you'll have to do a second batch.
3. Pour the tomato sauce over the meatballs without stirring.
4. Secure the lid and cook on high pressure for 5 minutes.
5. When time is up, let the pressure drop on its own.
6. Cut open a meatball to see if the rice is done. If it isn't tender yet, put the lid back on and let the meatballs cook in the left over heat.
7. Remove the meatballs and plate.
8. To thicken the sauce, mix cornstarch in one tablespoon of water and add to the pressure cooker.
9. Turn on the pressure cooker again on the lowest setting, and stir until the sauce gets thick enough.
10. Pour over your meatballs and serve.

Nutritional information (4 meatballs per serving):
Calories - 326
Protein- 16
Carbs - 17
Fat - 7
Fiber - 0

Cola-Braised Short Ribs

Serves: 4-6

Time: 1 hour, 50 minutes (40 minute cook time)

This recipe is the perfect marriage between spicy and sweet. The spice rub includes seasonings like paprika, cayenne pepper, and cumin, so you know you're going to get some heat from the beef. The cola helps sweeten things out a bit, and pressure cooking the ribs make them fall-off-the-bone tender.

Ingredients:

4 pounds English-cut beef short ribs (2 ½-inch pieces)
2 cups cola
6 smashed garlic cloves
½ diced yellow onion
2 tablespoons Worcestershire sauce
2 tablespoons soy sauce
2 tablespoons olive oil
2 tablespoons water
2 tablespoons cornstarch
2 teaspoons salt
2 teaspoons paprika
1 ½ teaspoons cayenne pepper
1 ½ teaspoons black pepper
½ teaspoon ground cumin

Directions:
1. Begin by preparing the spice rub. Combine paprika, salt, pepper, cumin, and cayenne in a bowl.
2. Rub unto the ribs.
3. In your pressure cooker, heat the olive oil and brown the ribs. Do not squeeze them in. The sear should take about 7 minutes.

4. Plate and repeat if necessary with the rest of the ribs.
5. Toss in the onion and garlic and soften.
6. Pour in the soy sauce, cola, and Worcestershire sauce and deglaze the pot.
7. Put the ribs back in the pressure cooker and coat them in the sauce.
8. Secure the lid and cook on high pressure for 40 minutes.
9. When the timer goes off, turn off the cooker and let the pressure come down on its own for 15 minutes.
10. Quick-release any remaining pressure.
11. Move the meat to a plate.
12. Strain the cooking liquid and remove any fat.
13. On the "sauté" setting, bring the liquid to a boil.
14. While the liquid is getting to the boil, mix the cornstarch and water together.
15. When smooth, pour half of the mixture into the cooker and whisk to thicken.
16. If necessary, add the rest of the cornstarch/water mixture.
17. Pour the sauce over the ribs and turn them with tongs to coat them evenly.
18. Serve and enjoy!

Nutritional information (per serving):
Calories - 868
Protein- 65
Carbs - 11
Fat - 58
Fiber - 0

Swiss Steak w/ Sauce
Serves: 4-6
Time: 25-30 minutes (15 minute cook time)

Tender, boneless beef round steak cooks together with a choir of veggies (carrots, celery, pepper, onion, carrots) in a delicious, tomato-soup based sauce seasoned with horseradish. This is a very easy recipe that only requires browning before everything cooks in the pot for 15 minutes.

Ingredients:
1 ½ pounds boneless beef round steak
1 can (10 ¾-ounces) condensed tomato soup
1 cup chopped green pepper
¾ cup chopped celery
2 chopped carrots
1 chopped onion
½ cup cold water
2 tablespoons flour
2 tablespoons canola oil
1 teaspoon horseradish
1 teaspoon cornstarch
½ teaspoon salt
¼ teaspoon pepper

Directions:
1. Cut the steak into bite-sized pieces and coat both sides in a mixture of flour, salt, and pepper.
2. Heat the oil in the pressure cooker before browning the steak on both sides.
3. Add the veggies.
4. In a separate bowl, mix the water and cornstarch.
5. Add the horseradish and soup and mix well.
6. Pour into the pressure cooker.
7. Secure the pressure cooker lid and cook on high pressure for 15 minutes.
8. When the timer goes off, quick-release the pressure.

Salisbury Steak

Serves: 4-6
Time: 1 hour (10 minute cook time)

Salisbury steak is when ground beef is shaped into the shape of a steak. It's easier to cook this way, and is famous being one of the first Swanson's TV dinners. This homemade version is so much better, it doesn't even compare.

Ingredients:
2 pounds ground beef
2 eggs
2 ½ cups beef stock
3 pressed garlic cloves
3 halved and sliced onions
1 cup breadcrumbs
2 tablespoons Worcestershire sauce
2 tablespoons olive oil
1 teaspoon dried parsley
1 teaspoon salt
½ teaspoon garlic powder
½ teaspoon black pepper
½ teaspoon onion powder
¼ teaspoon paprika
¼ teaspoon mustard powder

Directions:

1. Mix the beef, eggs, breadcrumbs, salt, pepper, onion powder, garlic powder, parsley, paprika, and 1 tablespoon of Worcestershire into patties with your hands. Make about 4-6, depending on how many people you're serving.
2. Heat 2 tablespoons of oil in your pressure cooker.
3. Brown the patties on both sides.
4. Plate the meat.
5. Sauté the cut onions until they are a little brown.
6. Throw in the garlic and sauté for another minute.
7. Add the second tablespoon of Worcestershire and beef stock.
8. Put the meat back in the cooker and sprinkle a little salt and pepper over the patties.
9. Secure the lid and cook on high pressure for 10 minutes.
10. Mix 1 tablespoon of cornstarch with 1 tablespoon of water. You will use this to thicken the gravy.
11. When time is up, turn off the cooker and let the pressure decrease naturally for 10 minutes.
12. Quick-release the rest of the pressure and remove the meat.
13. Turn the cooker back on the lowest heat setting and stir in the cornstarch mixture.
14. Stir for a few minutes until it thickens; do not bring to a boil.
15. When you're ready to serve, spoon the gravy over the steaks.
16. Serve with mashed potatoes, noodles, or with just side of veggies!

Nutritional information (per serving):

Calories - 339

Protein- 17.4
Carbs - 15.2
Fat - 22.8
Fiber - 1

Meaty Lasagna

Serves: 4-6

Time: 30 minutes (18 minute cook time)

This is the perfect lasagna. It's packed with a homemade meat sauce that uses 1 pound of ground beef chuck and savory seasonings like thyme, oregano, and garlic. You cook the whole thing in the pressure cooker - noodles included - so that for once in your life, lasagna is a one-pot meal.

<u>Ingredients:</u>
1 pound ground beef chuck
1 cup chopped tomatoes
1 finely-chopped onion
1 chopped celery stalk
1 chopped carrot
½ cup tomato puree
½ cup water
2 tablespoons unsalted butter
1 tablespoon olive oil
1 fresh thyme sprig
1 fresh oregano sprig
½ teaspoon salt
¼ teaspoon pepper
10 wavy lasagna noodles, broken into 2-inch pieces
8 ounces diced mozzarella
1 teaspoon salt
Water

Directions:

1. Let's start with the sauce. Turn your pressure cooker to "browning" and melt 1 tablespoon of butter with the olive oil.
2. Once the butter has melted, add the herbs, salt, pepper, and onion and sauté until softened.
3. Add the chopped celery and carrot.
4. With a spatula, scoot the veggies to the side of your cooker and add the beef and garlic.
5. Stir to break up the meat and brown for about 5 minutes.
6. Pour in the tomatoes.
7. Secure the pressure cooker lid and cook on high pressure for 18 minutes.
8. When time is up, quick-release the pressure.
9. Pick out the herb stems and melt the second tablespoon of butter into the sauce.
10. Now it's time for the lasagna.
11. Add salt and lasagna noodles to the sauce and pour in at least enough water to cover the noodles.
12. Close the lid again and cook on low pressure for 5 minutes.
13. Quick-release the pressure again.
14. If the noodles aren't tender, cook on simmer until ready.
15. Pour everything into a serving dish and sprinkle with the cheese.
16. Stir everything together again and let the food rest without a cover for 2 minutes before diving in.

Nutritional information (per serving):

Calories - 408

Protein- 24.9

Carbs - 43

Fat - 15

Fiber - 3.3

Seafood

Ginger White Fish w/ Orange

Serves: 4

Time: 17 minutes (7 minute cook time)

This is a great dinner idea if you only have a few ingredients on hand, but want to prepare a healthy, light dinner. The other nice thing about this recipe is that you can use any white fish. They are all mild-tasting and go perfectly with the orange and ginger.

Ingredients:

4 white fish fillets

3-4 spring onions

1 cup white wine

1 orange, juice and zest

Thumb-sized piece of ginger, chopped

Olive oil

Salt and pepper to taste

Directions:

1. Pat the fillets dry with a paper towel.
2. Rub olive oil on to the fish, and sprinkle with salt and pepper.
3. In your pressure cooker, pour in the stock, ginger, orange zest, juice, and onions.
4. Add the steamer basket with the fish fillets inside.

Cooking Tip

Because fish is so delicate, it must be cooked on LOW pressure. There are some exceptions, so always read the recipe carefully.

5.   Secure the pressure cooker lid and cook for 7 minutes on low pressure.
6.   Serve with a side of rice pilaf or on top of a salad.

Nutritional information (per serving):
Calories - 288
Protein- 50
Carbs - 2
Fat - 3
Fiber - 5

Salmon Al Cartoccio
Serves: 4
Time: 25 minutes (15 minute cook time)
"Al cartoccio" means "packet cooking" in Italian. In this recipe, you wrap everything in parchment paper and steam it in the pressure cooker, so the more delicate flavors are preserved, and the fish is fork-tender. You can do this same recipe with any kind of white fish, as well, and any kinds of spices and herbs.

Ingredients:
4 fresh salmon fillets
4 parsley sprigs
4 thyme sprigs
2 sliced potatoes
1 sliced lemon
1 shaved onion
Olive oil

Salt and pepper

<u>Directions:</u>
1. Lay down a sleeve of parchment paper.
2. Begin with a layer of olive oil, and then the following ingredients - potatoes, salt, pepper, olive oil, fish, salt, pepper, oil, herbs, onion, lemon, salt, and olive oil.
3. Fold the package carefully and then wrap in aluminum foil.
4. Prepare your pressure cooker with 2 cups of water and the steamer basket.
5. You can probably only fit two of the packets in the basket at once.
6. Once the packets are in the basket, cook on low pressure for 12-15 minutes.
7. Quick-release the pressure when time is up, but leave the packets in the cooker for another 5 minutes.
8. When you're ready to serve, carefully remove the packets and plate.

<u>Nutritional information (per serving):</u>
Calories - 310
Protein- 30
Carbs - 9
Fat - 14
Fiber - 3

Chilled Octopus & Potatoes
Serves: 6
Time: 55 minutes (35 minute cook time)

If you like to be adventurous in the kitchen, but are scared of ruining a unique ingredient, this is a great recipe to try out. It involves a whole octopus, and reliable ingredients like potatoes, garlic, and olive oil. Everything cooks in the pressure cooker, so you don't have to be worry too much about messing up the octopus.

Ingredients:
One 2-pound octopus
2 pounds potatoes
8 ½ tablespoons of olive oil
5 tablespoons vinegar
3 garlic cloves
1 bay leaf
½ teaspoon peppercorns
Chopped parsley
Salt and pepper to taste

Directions:
1. Begin by cleaning the octopus. Cut off its head and cut the body in half. Turn this part inside out and get rid of all the stuff inside, including the eyes and beak.
2. Rinse and plate.
3. Next, wash the potatoes and put them in the pressure cooker.
4. Add just enough water to cover the potatoes halfway up and sprinkle in salt.
5. Secure the lid and cook on high pressure for 15 minutes.
6. Quick-release the pressure and take out the potatoes. Leave the cooking liquid.
7. Peel the potatoes.
8. Pour more water into the cooker, so the octopus will be almost totally submerged.
9. Throw in the pepper, salt, bay leaf, and one garlic clove.

10. Bring the liquid to a boil before adding the octopus, tentacles down.
11. Close the lid and cook on high pressure for 20 minutes.
12. Quick-release the pressure and test the octopus. It should be fork-tender.
13. Strain the cooking liquid and cut the octopus into bite-sized pieces.
14. To make the vinaigrette, mix the vinegar, olive oil, 2 crushed garlic cloves, and salt and pepper.
15. Cut the potatoes into chunks like the octopus.
16. Combine all the ingredients, with parsley as a garnish. Chill covered in the fridge before eating.

Nutritional information (per serving):
Calories - 550
Protein- 48
Carbs - 39
Fat - 22
Fiber - 3

Pressure-Cooker Cod w/ Peas

Serves: 4
Time: 25 minutes (5 minute cook time)

Cod is one of the healthiest foods you could eat. It is also really low-calorie and high in protein; a 4-ounce fillet has 21 grams of protein. The pressure cooker is an extremely fast, efficient way to cook cod to a buttery tenderness. The mild flavors infused with herbs and spices go really well with peas.

Ingredients:
4 cod fillets
4 cups frozen peas
2 parsley sprigs
1 cup white wine

2 halved garlic cloves
½ teaspoon paprika
½ teaspoon dried oregano

Directions:
1. If the cod fillets are frozen, take out of the fridge and sit them out on the counter while you prepare the other ingredients.
2. In a food processor, chop the oregano, garlic, parsley, and paprika. Set aside for later.
3. Add the wine to the pressure cooker.
4. Put the fish fillets in the steamer basket and lower into the cooker.
5. Close the lid and cook on high pressure for 2 minutes.
6. When the timer goes off, quick-release the pressure and carefully plate the fish.
7. Add the peas to the cooker and close the lid.
8. Cook on high for 1 minute.
9. Quick-release the pressure again.
10. Serve the cod with the peas and then the herb mixture on top.

Nutritional information (per serving):
Calories - 263
Protein- 33
Carbs - 19
Fat - 1
Fiber - 7

Shrimp Alfredo
Serves: 4
Time: 12 minutes (10 minute cook time)

This rich, creamy pasta dish is made even more decadent when you introduce shrimp. This is a great dinner idea for a double date at home, or when you just want something special after your family has had a hard week at school and work.

Ingredients:
8 ounces bowtie pasta
2 ½ cups chicken broth
12 ounces uncooked, cleaned frozen shrimp
⅔cup diced red onion
1 cup grated parmesan
½ cup heavy cream
1 tablespoon minced garlic
1 tablespoon olive oil
1 teaspoon Old Bay seasoning
1 teaspoon flour
Salt and pepper
Parsley

Directions:
1. Heat the olive oil in your pressure cooker and sauté the onions until they become clear.
2. Add the pasta, chicken stock, garlic, old bay, and shrimp to the cooker.
3. Lock the lid and cook on high for 10 minutes.
4. Quick-release the pressure.
5. Add the parmesan, cream, flour, and salt and pepper.
6. Set the cooker to "brown" and simmer until the sauce is the way you want it.
7. Plate and garnish with fresh parsley.

Nutritional information (per serving):
Calories - 327
Protein- 26

Carbs - 34
Fat - 9
Fiber - 2

Shrimp Risotto w/ Herbs
Serves: 4
Time: 12 minutes (10 minute cook time)

This sophisticated risotto combines tender shrimp with fresh tarragon and parsley for a gourmet treat. It may sound intimidating, but the recipe doesn't actually have a long list of weird ingredients, and you can get the whole thing on the table in less than 15 minutes.

Ingredients:
1 pound cleaned shrimp
4 ½ cups chicken broth
1 ½ cups Arborio rice
4 tablespoons butter
2 minced garlic cloves
1 finely-chopped onion
¾ cup grated parmesan
¼ cup chopped tarragon and parsley
2 tablespoons dry white wine
Salt and pepper to taste

Directions:
1. Melt 2 tablespoons of butter and sauté the onion and garlic until they're soft.
2. Add the rice and stir for about 1 minute.
3. Pour in the wine and keep cooking until it evaporates, or about 30 seconds.
4. Add three cups of the broth and season with salt and pepper.

5. Close the lid and cook on high pressure for 10 minutes.
6. Quick-release the pressure.
7. Add the shrimp and the rest of the broth.
8. Cook for 5 minutes.
9. Add the cheese and the rest of the butter.
10. Stir in the herbs and serve right away!

Nutritional information (per serving):
Calories - 293.5
Protein- 25
Carbs - 19.5
Fat - 12.4
Fiber - 1.8

Tuna Pasta w/ Capers

Serves: 4-6
Time: 10 minutes (3 minute cook time)

It can be hard to know what to do with canned tuna, besides sandwiches. This recipe transforms ordinary canned tuna into a tasty pasta dish, complete with tomato sauce, capers, and anchovies. If you don't like anchovies, you can leave them out, of course.

Ingredients:
16-ounces fusilli pasta
2 (5.5-ounces) tuna packed in olive oil
3 anchovies
1 garlic clove
2 tablespoons capers
1 tablespoon olive oil
1 ½ teaspoons salt
Enough water to cover pasta

Directions:
1. Heat the oil in your pressure cooker.
2. Add the garlic and anchovies.
3. Cook until the garlic is beginning to turn golden, and the anchovies are falling apart.
4. Add the tomato puree and salt, and mix it all together.
5. Next, add the pasta and one tuna can.
6. Mix so the fish coats the pasta.
7. With a spatula, flatten the pasta down into one layer.
8. Pour in just enough water to cover the pasta before securing the pressure cooker lid.
9. Cook for 3 minutes on low pressure.
10. Quick-release the pressure and check the pasta. If it isn't tender enough, secure the lid again and cook for a few minutes more.
11. Quick-release.
12. When the pasta is done, add the last can of tuna and capers before eating.

Nutritional information (per serving):
Calories - 339.5
Protein- 20.5
Carbs - 51
Fat - 5.3
Fiber - 9

Homemade Fish Stock
Makes: 6 cups
Time: 35 minutes (30 minute cook time)

If you eat a lot of fish dishes, you want to be familiar with fish stock. This broth serves as the base for countless fish soups like chowder and fish sauces. For the fish parts, find a fish market where you can get fish heads and scraps, or get a whole fish (with the bones) and get rid of the gills.

Ingredients:
2 pounds of fish parts
6 cups water
4 peppercorns
1 celery stalk, cut into pieces
1 scraped carrot, cut into pieces
1 bay leaf
1 peeled and sliced onion
2 sprigs fresh parsley
1 teaspoon thyme
Salt to taste

Directions:
1. Throw everything into the pressure cooker.
2. Secure the lid and cook on high pressure for 30 minutes.
3. When the timer goes off, let the pressure come down by itself.
4. Open the lid and let the stock cool.
5. Strain so you get a smooth broth. Get rid of the solids.
6. Cover and store in the fridge or freeze.

Nutritional information (per serving):
Calories - 40
Protein- 5.3
Carbs - 0
Fat - 1.9
Fiber - 0

Pressure-Cooker Calamari

Serves: 4

Time: 45 minutes (30 minute cook time)

Calamari is squid, and is usually consumed deep-fried and bursting with calories and fat. This version is lighter and intended to be eaten as an appetizer. It can be served with spaghetti or rice. The pressure cooker ensures that the calamari isn't rubbery, but tender and delicious.

Ingredients:

1 ½ pounds calamari

14.5-ounce can of chopped tomatoes

1 smashed garlic clove

2 anchovies

1 juiced lemon

½ cup white wine

1 bunch of chopped parsley

Red pepper flakes

Olive oil

Salt and pepper to taste

Directions:

1. Begin by cleaning the calamari.
2. Gently pull off the squid helmet from the head, and run the helmet under water.
3. Pull off the skin and let the water clean out the insides.
4. You will feel a piece of cartilage; pull this out.
5. Cut the helmet into strips; they will look like rings.
6. For the tentacles, separate them from the eyes and pull out the beak by squeezing the sides and popping it out. The tentacles are ready to cook.

7. Heat 2 tablespoons of olive oil in the pressure cooker and sauté the garlic, anchovies, and pepper.
8. When the oil is hot, add the squid and cook for about 5 minutes.
9. Pour in the wine and wait 3 minutes.
10. Next, add the tomatoes.
11. Fill the tomato can with water and pour that in too, with half of the chopped parsley.
12. Secure the pressure cooker lid.
13. Cook on high pressure for about 25 minutes.
14. Quick-release the pressure when time is up.
15. Add the lemon juice, a splash of oil, and the fresh parsley.
16. Toss with cooked spaghetti, rice, or another side dish, like polenta.

Nutritional information (per serving):
Calories - 388
Protein- 40
Carbs - 18
Fat - 16
Fiber - 0

Quick New-England Clam Bake

Serves: 4
Time: 15 minutes (6 minute cook time)

Clam bakes are a classic New England dinner. Tons of seafood like lobster, clams, and scallops are cooked with herbs, potatoes, onions, and corn for the perfect summer "cook-out." They traditionally take hours and hours, but in a pressure cooker, it only takes 15-20 minutes!

Ingredients:

16-20 rinsed littleneck clams
10-ounce lobster tail
4-6 jumbo sea scallops
4 slivered garlic cloves
2-3 red potatoes cut into quarters
3 tablespoons butter
1 quartered onion
1 ½ cups water
1 bay leaf
1 tablespoon chopped herbs
Sea salt
1 ear of corn-on-the-cob, cut into 4 pieces
1 lemon

Directions:
1. Pour the water in your pressure cooker and toss in the herbs, garlic and bay leaf.
2. Season with salt and pepper.
3. Add the onion and potatoes.
4. Next, add the clams, spreading them evenly in the cooker.
5. Split the lobster in half, leaving the shell on, and season.
6. Put on top of the clams.
7. Season the sea scallops and put in the cooker.
8. Slice the butter and arrange on top of the scallops and lobster.
9. Lastly, add the corn.
10. Secure the lid and cook on high pressure for about 6 minutes.
11. Quick-release the pressure.
12. Serve right away with a lemon wedge for garnish.

Nutritional information (per serving):

Calories - 274
Protein- 24
Carbs - 40
Fat - 3
Fiber - 3

Whole Lobster in a Pressure Cooker

Serves: 2
Time: 7 minutes (3-4 minute cook time)

Whole lobster is a decadent dish. You have to steam the whole thing in the shell in boiling water. To go with the lobster, consider serving a good wine (like a white Burgundy) and a side like corn on the cob or steamed red potatoes.

Ingredients:
4 cups water
Two 2-pound lobster
2 strips dry seaweed

Directions:
1. In a saucepan, heat 4 cups of water until they are boiling.
2. Pour this water into the pressure cooker and add the dried seaweed.
3. Lower both lobsters into the pressure cooker so they are covered by the water.
4. Secure the pressure cooker lid and cook on high pressure for 3-4 minutes.
5. When time is up, unplug the cooker and quick-release the pressure.
6. Remove the lobster with a pair of tongs, and cut off the rubber bands.

Cooking Tip
You can tell the lobster is done when you can easily pull off one of the antennae. The meat inside will be white, solid, and firm.

7.   Serve right away and enjoy!

<u>Nutritional information (per serving):</u>
Calories - 171
Protein- 36
Carbs - 2
Fat - 2
Fiber – 0

Chapter 9 - Vegetarian Dishes

Spaghetti Squash Bake w/ Pesto and Parmesan

Serves: 4

Time: 30 minutes (8 minute cook time in pressure cooker)

Spaghetti squash is one of the tastiest and most versatile vegetables. You can substitute squash for noodles, and serve with a marinara sauce, or just brush the squash with olive oil and sprinkle on parmesan cheese and black pepper. It is higher in protein than pasta, and is lower in carbs. This recipe has you cook the spaghetti squash in a pressure cooker, and then bringing it all together in a regular oven for about 20 minutes.

Ingredients:

3-lb spaghetti squash

1 cup water

3 tablespoons pesto

1 ¼ cups Parmesan cheese

1 tablespoon olive oil

Salt and pepper

Directions:

1. Prepare the squash by cutting off the stem end and then cutting the squash in half lengthwise.
2. Spoon out the seeds.
3. Add water to the pressure cooker and put the squash in the steamer basket.
4. Cook for 8 minutes on high pressure.
5. Quick-release the pressure.
6. When the squash is cool enough to touch, scrap out the flesh with a fork into a bowl. It will resemble spaghetti strands (hence the name).

7. Mix the pesto and 1 cup of cheese into the squash, and season.
8. Pour this mixture into a gratin dish and sprinkle the last ¼ cup cheese on top.
9. Bake in a 400-degree oven for 20-30 minutes, or until the cheese is melty and golden.

Nutritional information (per serving):
Calories - 346
Protein- 17
Carbs - 31
Fat - 24
Fiber - 6

Indian Flatbread Pizza
Serves: 3
Time: 1 hour (30 minute cook time)

Pizza in a pressure cooker? It is possible. This Indian take on pizza uses wheat flour, herbs, onion, tomato, and bell peppers for a healthy supper. Because of how the pizza needs to cook, make sure you have a cooking pan or plate that won't touch the sides of the cooker when you lower it in.

Ingredients:
200 g of wheat flour (1 cup + 9 tablespoons flour)
¼ cup olive oil
1 big, sliced onion
1 sliced tomato
1 sliced bell pepper
¾ teaspoon baking powder
½ teaspoon sugar
¼ teaspoon salt
Cheese to taste

Herbs to taste
Chili flakes to taste
Tomato sauce to taste

Directions:
1.   In a bowl, mix the sugar, flour, salt, olive oil, and baking powder. Add a pinch of the herbs for flavor.
2.   Sprinkle water on the dough and knead into a smooth, round ball.
3.   Cover for 30 minutes.
4.   In the meantime, slice up your veggies.
5.   When 25 minutes has passed, preheat the pressure cooker.
6.   When the dough is ready, roll it into a pizza with an 8-9-inch diameter and ¼ inch thickness. If you find the dough is too sticky, add some flour.
7.   Prick holes with a fork down the entire dough, like you are drawing lines with the fork.
8.   Prepare the cooking pan with olive oil and put in the dough.
9.   After 5 minutes of preheating, put the trivet in the cooker, and then the cooking pan with the pizza.
10. Cover with a thick lid made of steel. You are not covering the pressure cooker for this recipe.
11. Cook on a low setting (like "browning") for 15 minutes.
12. Carefully remove the cooking pan and flip the pizza. Spread tomato sauce to taste and sprinkle on cheese and vegetables.
13. Return to the pressure cooker and cook for 15 more minutes on a low setting.
14. To check the dough, poke a knife through it, like you're testing a cake.
15. If the knife comes out clean, the dough is cooked.

16. Remove the pizza and plate. Sprinkle on herbs and chili flakes.

<u>Nutritional information (per serving):</u>
Calories - 577
Protein- 17
Carbs - 65
Fat - 29
Fiber - 4

Zucchini Pesto Sauce
Serves: 4
Time: 10 minutes (4 minute cook time)

For vegetarians, it can seem like they don't have a lot of sauce options that don't have animal stock. There's regular tomato sauce, but what else is there? This veggie-packed sauce uses both basil and zucchini as the base, and the bright green color is gorgeous any time of year. It's also a great way to use zucchini during its peak season, if you grow zucchini, because you probably have more than what you know what to do with.

<u>Ingredients:</u>
1 ½ pounds chopped zucchini
1 bunch of basil, w/ the leaves picked off
2 minced garlic cloves
3/4 cup water
2 tablespoons olive oil
1 ½ teaspoons salt
1 onion

<u>Directions:</u>
1. Heat the olive oil in your pressure cooker.
2. Sauté the onion until they are soft.

3. Add ¾ cup of water, salt, and the zucchini.
4. Secure the pressure cooker lid and cook on high pressure for about 4 minutes.
5. Quick-release the pressure. The zucchini should be very soft.
6. Add the garlic and basil.
7. In either a regular blender or with a hand blender, puree everything.
8. The pasta sauce is ready! Serve right away with the noodles of your choice and another twist of olive oil.

Nutritional information (per serving):
Calories - 71.4
Protein- 1.2
Carbs - 7.5
Fat - 4.7
Fiber - 2.3

Pressure-Cooker Mac 'n Cheese
Serves: 4-6
Time: 10 minutes (4 minute cook time)

Macaroni-and-cheese is one of childhood's favorite foods. It is everything that comfort food should be - hot, cheesy, and rich. Usually, homemade mac 'n cheese takes a lot longer than the kind in a box, so when you're crunched for time, you opt for the less healthy, more artificial. With a pressure cooker, you don't have to make that compromise.

Ingredients:
1 pound dried elbow macaroni pasta
4 cups water
1 (12-oz) can of evaporated milk
1 cup panko breadcrumbs

16 ounces shredded cheddar

6 ounces shredded Parmesan

2 tablespoons butter

1 tablespoon kosher salt

1 tablespoon yellow mustard

1 teaspoon hot pepper sauce

Directions:

1. In the pressure cooker, add the pasta, mustard, butter, hot sauce, salt, and 4 cups of water.

2. Secure the lid and cook on high pressure for 4 minutes.

3. Quick-release the pressure when time is up.

4. Next, put the cooker on "sauté," and stir in the evaporated milk.

5. If the pasta is still too chewy, simmer until it's tender.

6. Stir in the cheese (one handful at a time), waiting to add the next batch until the latter is melted.

7. For a toasty breadcrumb crust, pour the mac 'n cheese into a broiler-safe dish and top with panko.

8. Broil for 5 minutes and serve!

Nutritional information (per serving):

Calories - 349

Protein- 15.7

Carbs - 32

Fat - 17.3

Fiber - .8

Basic Pressure-Cooker Seitan

Serves: 8

Time: 40 minutes (35 minute cook time)

Seitan is a very popular meat substitute made from gluten, but it can be hard to make quite right. If you've ever made bread from scratch, seitan shouldn't be a problem. This recipe makes a flavorful, basic seitan that you can use in a variety of dishes in place of meat. It's flavored with fresh herbs like thyme and oregano, as well as liquid smoke and toasted sesame oil for deeper, richer tastes.

Ingredients:
1 ½ cups wheat gluten flour
¼ cup whole-grain flour
3 cups water
3 cups + 1 cup veggie broth
¼ cup tamari + 2 tablespoons tamari
2 tablespoons nutritional yeast
1 tablespoon minced shallots
2 teaspoons liquid smoke
1 teaspoon Worcestershire sauce
1 teaspoon toasted sesame oil
½ teaspoon thyme
½ teaspoon garlic powder
½ teaspoon oregano
Salt to taste

Directions:
1. First, whisk the dry ingredients together.
2. In a separate bowl, whisk everything else together (except any of the broth).
3. Add the wet to the dry and stir.
4. Knead well for 5 minutes and shape a log that's about 8 inches long and 2 inches thick.
5. Wrap this in a cheesecloth and tie the ends closed with kitchen string.

6. Pour in all the broth into the pressure cooker on a low setting until it boils.
7. Add the log and close the lid.
8. Cook on high for 30-35 minutes.
9. When the timer goes off, wait for the pressure to decrease on its own.
10. Open the lid and set out the log. Do not unwrap it yet.
11. After a few more minutes, unwrap and slice the log into strips.
12. You can store these strips in a container in a fridge with a little bit of the cooking liquid, so it doesn't dry out.

Nutritional information (per serving):
Calories - 195
Protein- 26.1
Carbs - 15.6
Fat -2.1
Fiber - 1.6

Curried Potatoes, Cauliflower, and Peas

Serves: 6
Time: 10 minutes (5 minute cook time)

If you haven't been using Indian spices in your cooking, you are really missing out on how good vegetables can taste. Simple potatoes, cauliflower, and peas transform into an aromatic, multi-layered marriage of flavors from the ginger, curry, and turmeric. You can serve this as a side dish or as a lunch option. Toppings include cold plain Greek yogurt, rice, or cucumber raita, which is kind of like an Indian twist on coleslaw. The recipe for the raita is also included below.

Ingredients:
6 Yukon gold potatoes, cut into ½-inch bits

2 cups chopped onion
1 cored and cut cauliflower (1-inch pieces)
1 cup thawed frozen peas
4 minced garlic cloves
2 teaspoons melted butter
2 teaspoons minced ginger
1 ½ teaspoons curry powder
1 teaspoon sugar
1 teaspoon brown mustard seeds
1 teaspoon ground cumin
½ teaspoon ground turmeric

Directions:
1. Heat the butter in your pressure cooker.
2. Sauté the onions until they are soft.
3. Add the ginger, cumin, turmeric, mustard seeds, curry, and garlic and sauté for another 2 minutes.
4. Throw in the sugar, ½ cup water, potatoes, and cauliflower.
5. Secure the pressure cooker lid and cook on high pressure for about 5 minutes.
6. Quick-release the pressure.
7. Add the peas and season with salt and pepper. Serve hot!

To make the cucumber raita:
1. Peel and cut 1 medium cucumber into lengthwise strips about ¼-inch, and then cut again crosswise.
2. Toast 1 teaspoon cumin seeds in a small frying pan.
3. Stir 2 cups plain, whole-milk yogurt, and then add 1 minced garlic clove, the cumin seeds, and 2 tablespoons chopped mint leaves.
4. Add the cucumber strips and season with cayenne (or paprika) to your liking.

Nutritional information (per serving, not including raita):
Calories - 184
Protein- 7
Carbs - 35
Fat - 2
Fiber - 6

BBQ Tofu
Serves: 6
Time: 12 minutes (5 minute cook time)

Tofu is a food made from soybeans and is commonly used in Japanese cuisine. It's high in nutrition, low in calories, and also pretty cheap! Because it has such a mild taste, it can be seasoned and cooked just about any way, and turn out great. This recipe adds BBQ sauce to the mix. I'm not going to lie and say you will think you're eating meat, but you'll definitely enjoy its substitute!

Ingredients:
28 ounces of cubed extra-firm tofu
12-ounces BBQ sauce of your choice
4 peeled and minced garlic cloves
1 chopped onion
1 diced red bell pepper
1 diced green bell pepper
1 diced celery stalk
2 tablespoons olive oil
Pinch of curry powder
Salt to taste

Directions:
1. Heat the olive oil in your electric pressure cooker.

2. Toss in the peppers, onion, garlic, and celery and season with the curry powder and salt.
3. Sauté for 2 minutes.
4. Add the tofu and cook for another 5 minutes while stirring.
5. Pour in the BBQ sauce.
6. Secure the lid and cook on high for 5-6 minutes.
7. Quick-release the pressure.
8. Open the lid and spoon the tofu onto a bed of hot rice.
9. Enjoy!

Nutritional information (per serving, without rice):
Calories - 207.7
Protein- 14.4
Carbs - 14.1
Fat - 11.6
Fiber - 2.6

Sweet Potatoes w/ Poached Eggs
Serves: 4
Time: 35 minute (14 minute cook time)

This sweet potato recipe is a great idea for a simple brunch, especially when you add in the poached egg. Sweet potatoes are also very healthy, with a high amount of vitamin A, vitamin C, and antioxidants. A poached egg adds protein and the yolk serves as a delicious sauce for the potato flesh.

Ingredients:
4 sweet potatoes
Water
4 poached eggs
Salt and pepper to taste

Directions:

1. Prepare the sweet potatoes by washing them and piercing them with a fork.
2. Pour one cup of boiling water into the pressure cooker and lower in the steaming basket. The water should be *below* the rack.
3. Put the potatoes in the steamer basket; they should not be touching the water.
4. For small potatoes, cook for 14 minutes on high pressure.
5. Turn off the pressure cooker and let the pressure decrease on its own for 10 minutes.
6. Quick-release the remaining pressure.
7. Poke the potato with a fork; they should be soft all the way through.
8. If they are ready, bake the potatoes in an oven for 10-15 minutes.
9. When there is about 3-4 minutes left for the potatoes in the oven, make the poached eggs.
10. Cut the sweet potatoes open, making a little hollow for the eggs.
11. Using a slotted spoon, carefully move the eggs to the sweet potatoes.
12. Season with salt and pepper!

Nutritional information (per serving):
Calories - 125
Protein- 7
Carbs - 12
Fat - 5
Fiber - 2

Allspice Eggplants w/ Feta + Pomegranate
Serves: 6

Time: 10 minutes (6 minute cook time)

Eggplants are high in fiber and are considered a "brain food," which means they are full of nutrients that help protect the cells in your brain from damage. While a lot of people don't like eggplant because it can taste bitter, the pomegranate molasses in this recipe helps sweeten the vegetable. Other spices like ground allspice, cinnamon, and fresh mint all add depth, as well, making this dish a full-flavored, hearty meal for vegetarians .

Ingredients:
6 Japanese eggplants, sliced into 1-inch rounds
1 ½ cups cooked chickpeas
1 (15-ounce) can of diced tomatoes
2 cups chopped onion
½ cup fresh pomegranate seeds
1/3 cup chopped fresh mint
¼ cup crumbled feta cheese
1 tablespoon roasted garlic olive oil
1 tablespoon pomegranate molasses
1 ¼ teaspoons Aleppo pepper
½ teaspoon ground allspice
¼ teaspoon ground cinnamon

Directions:
1. Heat the olive oil in your pressure cooker.
2. When hot, add the onions, cinnamon, allspice, and Aleppo to soften.
3. When the onions are soft, add the sliced eggplant, tomatoes (with the juice), pomegranate molasses, and chickpeas.
4. Stir until everything is well combined.

5. Secure the pressure cooker lid and cook on high pressure for 6 minutes.
6. Quick-release the pressure.
7. The eggplant should be tender, but not soggy.
8. Season with salt and pepper if necessary.
9. Move to a bowl and crumble on the feta before adding the pomegranate seeds and mint leaves.

Nutritional information (per serving):
Calories - 193
Protein- 8
Carbs - 33
Fat - 5
Fiber - 11

Vegetarian Reisfleisch

Serves: 8
Time: 1 hour, 10 minutes (15 minute cook time)

Reisfleisch, which translates to "rice flesh," is usually a rice stew that uses ham or pork, but this vegetarian version loads up on the veggies. The meal is best when the vegetables are fresh, of course, you can use frozen vegetables too if you want a taste of summer during the colder months.

Ingredients:
2 ¼ cups veggie stock
2 cups long-grain brown rice
1 ½ cups broccoli florets
1 ½ cups frozen peas
1 ½ cups asparagus, cut into 1-inch pieces
1 ½ cups green beans, cut into 1-inch pieces
1 ½ cups carrot
1 ½ cups diced yellow onion

1 ½ cups celery
1 ½ cups diced red bell pepper
2 minced garlic cloves
2 tablespoons parsley
1 tablespoon butter
1 tablespoon sweet paprika
2 teaspoons lemon juice
1 teaspoon red pepper flakes
Salt and pepper to taste

Directions:
1. Preheat the pressure cooker.
2. Once warm, melt the butter and wait till it starts to darken.
3. Quickly add the onion, celery, carrot, garlic, and bell pepper and sauté.
4. When they are beginning to soften, pour in the stock, rice, lemon juice, red pepper flakes, paprika, salt, and pepper.
5. Stir well.
6. Secure the pressure cooker lid and set the timer for 12 minutes on high pressure.
7. When the timer goes off, turn off the cooker and let the pressure come down on its own for 10 minutes.
8. Quick-release the rest of the pressure.
9. Add the frozen peas, green beans, broccoli, and asparagus.
10. With a fork, mix the veggies so they are nicely integrated into the rice.
11. Close the lid again and cook on a low setting for 3 minutes so the frozen veggies heat up.
12. Serve the stew with parsley.

Nutritional information (per serving):

Calories - 145
Protein- 7
Carbs - 26
Fat - 2
Fiber - 5

Homemade Veggie Stock
Makes: 8-10 cups
Time: 15 minutes (10 minute cook time)

Veggie stock is a must for vegetarians and vegans alike. If you don't want to use water for every recipe in place of the usual chicken, beef, and fish stock, you'll have to use store-bought or homemade veggie stock. Homemade stock is extremely cheap to make, and with a pressure cooker, takes only 10 minutes of cooking time.

<u>Ingredients:</u>
8 cups water
1 gallon freezer bag of vegetable scraps, like mushrooms stems, zucchini, asparagus stems, onion peels and scraps, lettuce, radishes, etc.
2 bay leaves
1 teaspoon olive oil
½ teaspoon of rosemary
½ teaspoon thyme
½ teaspoon oregano
½ teaspoon salt

Cooking Tip
If you have a bunch of frozen vegetables that you don't know what to do with, these are great for stock, too.

Directions:
1. Thaw the frozen veggies.
2. When thawed, chop them up into small bits.
3. Add the water and olive oil to your pressure cooker and heat.
4. Add the salt and spices.
5. Toss the veggies into the pressure cooker and cook on high pressure for 10 minutes.
6. When the timer goes off, unplug and let the pressure come down naturally.
7. When the stock is a little cooler, strain through a cheesecloth-lined sieve, squeezing the veggies with a pair of tongs to get all the juice out.
8. Discard the solids.
9. Store in the fridge or freezer.

Nutritional information (1 cup per serving):
Calories - 70
Protein- 2
Carbs - 16
Fat - 0
Fiber – 2

Chapter 10 - Vegan Dishes

Fresh Beet Salad
Serves: 4-6
Time: 35 minutes (30 minute cook time)

Beets are a uniquely-healthy vegetable and provide anti-inflammatory, antioxidant, and detox benefits. This simple steamed vegan salad is just beets, balsamic vinegar, and seasonings.

Ingredients:
4 whole beets
2 tablespoons white balsamic vinegar
2 tablespoons capers
1 tablespoon extra virgin olive oil
1 heaping tablespoon chopped parsley
1 garlic clove
Salt and pepper to taste

Directions:
1. Pour 1 cup of water into the pressure cooker and insert the steamer basket.
2. Clean and snip the tops of the beets.
3. Place beets in the steamer basket.
4. Secure the lid, and cook on high pressure for 20-25 minutes.
5. Meanwhile, make the dressing.
6. Chop the garlic and parsley, and shake in a small jar along with salt, pepper, capers, and olive oil to blend really well.
7. Quick-release the pressure cooker. You know the beets are done if easily pierced.
8. Run cold water over the beets and brush the skin off.

9. Slice the beets into discs.
10. Plate and dress.
11. If you aren't eating the beets right away, just spray them with a little vinegar and store in a tightly-closed container.

Nutritional information (per serving):
Calories - 43.1
Protein- 0.7
Carbs - 5.4
Fat - 2.4
Fiber - .8

Steamed Artichokes w/ Dijon Mustard

Serves: 4
Time: 25 minutes (15 minute cook time)

Artichokes are most commonly found in artichoke dip, which is full of calories and fat, but they are actually a very healthy vegetable. They contain vitamin C, antioxidants, and fiber. If you haven't eaten steamed artichokes before, the heart is the most delicious part. I've included a simple vegan mayo recipe, no charge.

Ingredients:
2 large artichokes, cut in half
2 tablespoons vegan mayo
1 teaspoon Dijon
1 sliced lemon
1 pinch paprika

Directions:
1. Trim and wash the artichokes, removing any damaged leaves and spines.

2. If you cut any part of the artichoke, rub with the lemon half, like you would to keep apples from browning.
3. Slice off the stem (if it has one) to create a flat bottom.
4. Pour 1 cup of water into your pressure cooker.
5. Put in the artichokes, facing up, and squeeze more lemon juice on them.
6. Secure the pressure cooker lid.
7. Cook for 15 minutes on high pressure.
8. Let the pressure come down naturally for 10 minutes, then quick-release the rest.
9. If you can easily bite into a leaf, they're done.
10. Make the dipping sauce by mixing the mayo with mustard and paprika.

To make vegan mayo:
1. *Mix ½ cup soy milk with 1 teaspoon fresh lemon juice in a blender for 30 seconds.*
2. *While it blends, slowly add 1 cup of olive oil until it combines and becomes thicker.*
3. *Season with a pinch of salt and ground mustard as you finish blending.*

Nutritional information (½ artichoke per serving):
Calories - 77.5
Protein- 2
Carbs - 0
Fat - 5
Fiber - 3.5

Vegan Refried Beans
Serves: 4 (as a side)
Time: 20 minutes (15 minute cook time)

Refried beans are creamy, packed with fiber and protein, and great with Mexican rice and a swirl of olive oil.

Ingredients:
2 cups dried, soaked pinto beans
2 cups water
1 chopped onion
1 bunch chopped parsley, stems separated from leaves
1 tablespoon olive oil
1 teaspoon salt
½ teaspoon cumin
¼ teaspoon chipotle powder

Directions:
1. Heat the oil in your pre-heated pressure cooker.
2. Sauté the parsley stems, onion, cumin, and chipotle.
3. When the onions are beginning to soften, add the water and beans.
4. Secure the lid and cook on high pressure for 7-10 minutes.
5. When ready, unplug the cooker and wait for 10 minutes.
6. Quick-release any remaining pressure before opening the lid.
7. Season with salt, and mash the beans with a potato masher.
8. Serve with a garnish of parsley!

Nutritional information (per serving):
Calories - 241
Protein- 15.8
Carbs - 44.1
Fat - .7
Fiber - 10.8

Marsala Potatoes

Serves: 3-4
Time: 18 minutes (8 minute cook time)

These are no ordinary potatoes. They are cooked in sweet dry wine and seasoned to perfection with rosemary, olive oil, and salt - a potato's best friends. These are a great side dish and snack, if there are any leftovers.

Ingredients:
4-5 medium diced potatoes
1 cup of Marsala wine
1 sprig rosemary
Olive oil
Salt and pepper

Directions:
1. Wash and scrub the potatoes. Leave the skins on.
2. Dice the potatoes.
3. Heat some olive oil in your pressure cooker and add the salt, pepper, rosemary sprig, and potatoes.
4. Move around and cook in the pan for 5 minutes.
5. Pour in the wine and deglaze the pot.
6. Close the lid and cook on high for 6-7 minutes.
7. Quick-release the pressure.
8. The potatoes will be tender and easily pierced with a fork.

Nutritional information (per serving):
Calories - 279
Protein- 13
Carbs - 45
Fat – 6

Caribbean Beans + Rice

Serves: 6
Time: 40 minutes (30 minute cook time)

Beans and rice are one of the healthiest food combinations there is, because they form a complete protein. For vegans, having good sources of protein is very important since they aren't getting that from meat. This Caribbean twist on the classic combines spicy and sweet from a hot pepper and coconut.

Ingredients:
2 cups boiling water
1 ½ cups long-grained brown rice
1 cup firm cooked black-eyed peas
1 chopped onion
1 seeded and chopped chili pepper
1 diced red pepper
1 (15-ounce) can diced tomatoes
½ cup dried unsweetened coconut
1 tablespoon olive oil
¼ cup fresh cilantro
2 teaspoons minced garlic
½ teaspoon salt
½ teaspoon dried thyme

Directions:
1. Heat the olive oil in your pressure cooker and sauté the garlic, onion, and chili pepper for about a minute.
2. Next, add the tomatoes, rice, coconut, thyme, salt, red pepper, and water.

3. Secure the pressure cooker lid and cook on high pressure for 30 minutes.
4. When time is up, let the pressure come down on its own for 10 minutes.
5. Quick-release any leftover pressure.
6. Stir in the beans and cilantro.
7. Wait a few minutes before serving, so the beans can warm up.

Nutritional information (per serving):
Calories - 165
Protein- 5.9
Carbs - 29
Fat - 2.8
Fiber - 6.1

Rice Pilaf w/ Carrots, Peas, and Almonds
Serves: 8-10
Time: 15 minutes (3 minute cook time)

This fluffy, veggie-packed pilaf is a fantastic side to compliment dinner, even for your non-vegan friends and family. The recipe originally called for both butter and chicken broth, but I've substituted them out for olive oil and veggie stock.

Ingredients:
2 cups rinsed long-grain white rice
1 ¼ cups of water
1 (14-ounce) can of veggie broth
1 cup thawed frozen peas
1 chopped onion
1 chopped carrot
1 chopped celery

½ cup toasted, sliced almonds
2 tablespoons chopped parsley
1 tablespoon olive oil
½ teaspoon salt

Directions:
1. Heat the olive oil in your pressure cooker.
2. Add the celery, carrots, and onions and sauté until the veggies are tender.
3. Add the rice and cook for 1-2 minutes.
4. Pour in the water, broth, and salt.
5. Secure the pressure cooker lid and cook on high for 3 minutes.
6. When time is up, wait 5 minutes before doing a quick-release.
7. Using a fork to fluff, add in the parsley, almonds, and peas.

Nutritional information (per serving):
Calories - 114
Protein- 4
Carbs - 17
Fat - 3
Fiber - 3

Asian Split-Pea Soup
Serves: 3
Time: 30 minutes (10 minute cook time)

Classic split-pea soup gets an Asian makeover with flavors like ginger, Shoyu soy sauce, and toasted sesame oil. Some of the ingredients, like the whole star anise flowers, are a little tricky to find, but if you have an Asian food market in your area, I'm sure they will have what you're looking for.

Ingredients:
10 small dried shiitake mushrooms
2 cups boiling water
4 cups water
2 whole star anise flowers
5 sliced scallions, with the white and green parts separated
2-3 cups watercress leaves, chopped
5-inch thumb of ginger
1 ½ cups rinsed split peas
1 cup onion
¼ cup dry sherry
1-3 tablespoons Japanese soy sauce (Shoyu)
1 tablespoon peanut oil
1 tablespoon toasted black sesame seeds
2 teaspoons minced garlic
½ teaspoon salt
2 teaspoons Asian toasted sesame oil

Directions:
1. Put the mushrooms and star anise in a big glass measuring cup and pour 2 cups of boiling water over them.
2. Cover and set aside for about 10 minutes.
3. When the mushrooms are tender, use a slotted spoon to get them and the star anise out.
4. Cut the mushrooms caps (getting rid of the stems) and set the shiitake, star anise, and liquid aside for later.

5. In your pressure cooker (6-quart minimum), heat the oil.
6. Put in the white part of the scallions, garlic, and onion and sauté until they are softened.
7. Pour in the sherry and stir until the sherry evaporates.
8. Pour in the 4 cups of water, sliced shiitake, split peas, star anise, and salt.
9. Lastly, add the soaking liquid.
10. Secure the lid and cook on high pressure for 10 minutes.
11. While this cooks, trim and grate the ginger root.
12. When you have a tablespoon, press down to get the juice out.
13. When the timer goes off, leave the pressure to come down on its own.
14. Add the scallion greens, watercress, soy sauce, sesame oil, and ginger juice.
15. Serve hot with the black sesame seeds as a garnish.

Nutritional information (per serving):
Calories - 291
Protein- 11
Carbs - 34
Fat - 10
Fiber - 2

Eggplant Caponata
Serves: 4-6 (side dish)
Time: 1 hour, 5 minutes (2 minute cook time)

A "caponata" is a Sicilian eggplant dish that has been around for centuries. This recipe is a fairly traditional take, with the eggplant cooked with celery in a sweet and sour sauce that includes raisins, balsamic vinegar, and other spices. The time calls for an hour and 5 minutes, with the hour needed for the eggplant cubes to sit out and drain some of their moisture.

Ingredients:
1 pound of peeled and cubed eggplant, about ½-inch cubes
4 pureed plum tomatoes
3 sliced celery ribs , ¼-inch
2 chopped garlic cloves
1 chopped onion
1 seeded and diced red bell pepper
½ cup pitted, oil-cured olives
⅓cup raisins
¼ cup balsamic vinegar
¼ cup minced parsley
1 tablespoon capers
1-2 tablespoons olive oil
½ teaspoon salt
¼ teaspoon ground cinnamon
Salt and pepper to taste

Directions:
1. Prepare the eggplant cubes by seasoning with salt and putting them in a colander atop a plate. Put a kitchen towel on top and then a weight.
2. Let this sit undisturbed on the counter for 1 hour.
3. When time is up, squeeze the eggplant (using the towel) to drain out any remaining moisture.
4. In your pressure cooker, heat the olive oil.
5. Sauté the onion and garlic for about 1 minute.

6. Add the eggplant, red pepper, olives, raisins, capers, and celery.
7. In a separate container, mix the vinegar, cinnamon and pureed tomatoes.
8. Pour this over the vegetables, and season with salt and pepper.
9. Close the pressure cooker lid and cook on high pressure for about 2 minutes.
10. Quick-release the pressure.
11. Test the tenderness of the eggplant, and cover again (without turning on) to finish steaming in the leftover heat.
12. Add any seasonings if necessary before serving.
13. Garnish with the chopped parsley and enjoy!

Nutritional information (per ½ cup serving):
Calories - 110
Protein- 1
Carbs - 8
Fat - 7
Fiber - 2

Chickpea Curry + Brown Rice

Serves: 4
Time: 30 minutes (20 minute cook time)

Chickpeas are one of the best vegan protein sources, with 15 grams per cup. They also have high amounts of potassium and fiber, and leave you feeling full. Because of their natural mild flavor, they take to just about any spice, like in this tasty curry and brown rice medley.

Ingredients:
2 ¼ cups water

1 ½ cups brown rice

2 cups water

1 cup quick-soaked chickpeas

1 large handful of whole, cherry tomatoes

1 chopped red onion

2 tablespoons chana masala spice mix

1 tablespoon minced garlic

1 tablespoon olive oil

1 tablespoon minced ginger

1 teaspoon salt

Directions:

1. Pour 2 ¼ cups of water and rice into a pressure-cooker safe container.
2. In your pressure cooker, heat the oil and sauté the onion until it starts to caramelize. This should take about 7 minutes.
3. Add the garlic, chana masala, and ginger. Sauté for 30 seconds or until the garlic becomes aromatic.
4. Pour in 2 cups water, tomatoes, and chickpeas into the cooker.
5. Lower the container (uncovered) with the rice and water into the steamer basket.
6. Secure the pressure cooker lid and cook on high pressure for 20 minutes.
7. When the timer beeps, unplug and wait until the pressure comes down naturally.
8. After 10 minutes, quick-release any leftover pressure.
9. Plate the rice first, and then add the curry mixture and mix.

Nutritional information (per serving):

Calories - 393

Protein- 10.9

Carbs - 74
Fat - 7
Fiber - 10.2

Nutmeg & Sage Butternut Squash Risotto

Serves: 4-6
Time: 20 minutes (15 minute cook time)

When autumn starts to deepen into winter, butternut squash reaches its peak. This full-bodied, mildly-sweet vegetable is one of my favorites, and goes so well with the nutmeg and sage in this recipe. It is the perfect accompaniment to arborio rice risotto and creates a filling, yet light dish.

Ingredients:
4 cups of diced butternut squash
4 cups water
2 cups arborio rice
4 whole garlic cloves
2 tablespoons olive oil
2 sage sprigs, leaves cut off
¼ cup white wine
2 teaspoons sea salt
1 teaspoon ground nutmeg

Directions:
1. Heat the olive oil in your pressure cooker.
2. Throw in the sage leaves and garlic.
3. When the sage leaves start to crisp up, take out a few of them for the garnish.
4. When the garlic turns golden, remove these as well and set aside.
5. Add the squash so a single layer covers the bottom.

6.	Move them around so they become coated with the sage and olive oil.
7.	Do not touch the squash as one side browns up.
8.	After 4 minutes, push the cubes to one side and add the rice.
9.	Toast for a few minutes.
10.	Add the wine and wait until it evaporates.
11.	Add the rest of the squash, garlic, salt, and water.
12.	Mix and secure the pressure cooker lid.
13.	Cook for 5 minutes on high pressure.
14.	Quick-release.
15.	Serve right away with some nutmeg and the crispy sage leaves you took out from earlier.

Nutritional information (1 cup per serving):
Calories - 311.9
Protein- 5.7
Carbs - 61.2
Fat - 5
Fiber - 3.9

Sweet Potato Jackfruit Enchiladas

Serves: 10-12
Time: 40 minutes (30 minute cook time)

This is a great recipe for vegans who sometimes find themselves missing meat. The jackfruit has a very meat-like texture, and with spices like chili powder, taco seasoning, and cumin, it has a very meat-like taste, too! Sweet potatoes add some heft to the recipe with vegan cheese rounding everything out.

Ingredients:
10-12 corn tortillas

1 (17-ounce) can of rinsed and drained jackfruit packed in water

1 (12-ounce can) red enchilada sauce

4 diced garlic cloves

1 (4-ounce) can diced green chilies

1 (2.25-ounce) can sliced black olives

Enough veggie broth to cover potatoes and jackfruit

¾ cup diced sweet potato

¼ diced onion

2 teaspoons taco seasoning

1 teaspoon extra virgin olive oil

1 teaspoon cumin

1 teaspoon chili powder

¼ teaspoon sea salt

Shredded vegan cheddar cheese

Directions:
1. Heat the oil in your pressure cooker and sauté the garlic and onion for a few minutes.
2. Add the sweet potatoes and continuing sautéing.
3. After a few minutes, add the veggie broth, salt, chili powder, cumin, taco seasoning, and the jackfruit.
4. Stir well before securing the lid on the pressure cooker.
5. Cook on high pressure for 10 minutes.
6. Quick-release the pressure.
7. Stir the potatoes and jackfruit. The potatoes should be mushy, and you should be able to shred the jackfruit with a fork.
8. In a saucepan, heat the enchilada sauce.
9. Coat the corn tortillas in the sauce for 20-30 seconds and plate.
10. Take the saucepan off the heat.
11. Fill the tortillas with a tablespoon of the jackfruit/potato mixture, spreading it in the middle.

12. Add the black olives and chilies before rolling tightly.
13. Place them seam-side down on a greased glass baking dish.
14. Pour the rest of the sauce over the enchiladas
15. Sprinkle with the vegan cheese and any leftover chilies and olives.
16. Bake at 350-degrees in the oven for 20 minutes.

Nutritional information (per serving):
Calories - 123
Protein- 3
Carbs - 23
Fat - 2
Fiber – 3

Chapter 11 - Desserts

Pepper-Jelly Lemon Cheesecake
Serves: 4-6 (depends on size of slices)
Time: 25 minutes (15 minute cook time)

I bet you never thought you would see the words "pepper jelly" go before "lemon cheesecake." This spicy, sweet, and tangy dessert might sound really fancy and difficult, but in the pressure cooker, it's really not hard at all and the whole thing is done in less than a half hour. If you're looking for a little adventure in the kitchen, this is a great dessert to try.

Ingredients:
2 cups macaroon cookies
6 sheets of graham crackers
2 tablespoons butter
16-ounces of room temperature cream cheese
2 (smallish) eggs
½ cup white sugar
1 tablespoon lemon zest
1 ½ tablespoons fresh lemon juice
1-2 tablespoons Habanero pepper jelly (if this is your first time making this, I recommend going easy on the jelly until you know you like it)
1 teaspoon vanilla

Directions:
1. Put the cookies and graham crackers into a food processor and run until they are crumbled.
2. Add the butter and continue processing until they're more clumped.
3. A springform pan is ideal. Grease the sides and bottom of the pan with butter.

4. Pack in the crumb mixture until you get a thick bottom crust that's about 1-inch high.
5. Now, let's make the filling.
6. Beat the cream cheese with the sugar.
7. Add the other ingredients and carefully blend until everything is smooth and incorporated.
8. Pour into the crust and smooth evenly.
9. Prepare the pressure cooker with 2-3 cups of water.
10. Put a trivet in the pot.
11. Wrap the pan with foil and place on top of the trivet.
12. Secure the pressure cooker lid and cook on high for 15 minutes.
13. When time is up, let the pressure come down on its own.
14. Turn off the pressure cooker and leave the cheesecake in the pot before trying to remove it - it's hot.
15. Cool the cheesecake in the fridge for at least an hour or until the cheesecake looks more set.
16. Remove it from the pan and serve!

Nutritional information (per serving):
Calories - 639
Protein- 10
Carbs - 43
Fat - 48
Fiber - 0

Pressure-Cooker Chocolate Pudding
Serves: 6
Time: 31 minutes (20 minute cook time)

Cold chocolate pudding takes me back to my childhood. In those days, the pudding came in a little plastic cup and was packed with artificial ingredients, but this pressure-cooker version uses quality ingredients like dark chocolate and pure vanilla. It is a refreshing, rich treat that won't make you feel guilty.

Ingredients:
1 ¼ cups chopped dark chocolate
1 ¼ cups fresh, plain breadcrumbs
½ cup condensed milk
½ cup milk
2 tablespoons softened butter
1 tablespoon powdered sugar

Directions:
1. In a double boiler, melt the dark chocolate and milk. Stir until it's smooth.
2. In a bowl, combine the chocolate with the vanilla, bread crumbs, butter, sugar, and condensed milk
3. Divide the mixture into two batches.
4. Pour one batch into a greased aluminum tin and cover loosely with foil.
5. In the pressure cooker, put down the trivet and a sieve on top of that.
6. Pour in the minimum water required for your specific cooker.
7. Put the chocolate tin on the sieve.
8. Pressure cook on high for 20 minutes.
9. Wait until the pressure goes down by itself.
10. Make the second batch.
11. Both puddings should be stored in the fridge for at least half an hour before eating.

Nutritional information (per serving):
Calories - 165
Protein- 2.7
Carbs - 31.7
Fat - 3.6
Fiber - .6

Gingered Applesauce

Serves: 4
Time: 15 minutes (4 minute cook time)

Regular homemade applesauce is great as is - it's a relatively healthy yet sweet snack, it's perfect during fall when apples are cheap and aplenty, and everyone loves it. This pressure-cooker recipe adds some crystallized ginger, which adds a spice similar to cinnamon, but wholly unique.

Ingredients:
4 pounds chopped apples
3-4 tablespoons crystallized ginger
½ cup water

Directions:
1. Pour the water into the pressure cooker.
2. Add the apples and ginger.
3. Cook on high pressure for 4 minutes.
4. Turn off the cooker and wait until the pressure has gone down, which should be about 10 minutes.
5. Stir the applesauce mixture until it looks the way you want, or use a hand blender if you want it to be really smooth.
6. Store in glass jars or another container for up to 10 days in the fridge.

Nutritional information (1 cup per serving):
Calories - 258
Protein- 5
Carbs - 66
Fat - 1
Fiber - 5.5

Molten Lava Cake

Serves: 2
Time: 12 minutes (8 minute cook time)

Is there any better date-night dessert than a molten lava cake? It's often a staple at upscale eateries, but now you can make it at home in your pressure cooker in just over 10 minutes! Serve with fresh raspberries, strawberries, and/or homemade whipped cream.

Ingredients:
½ cup semi-sweet chocolate chips
¼ cup powdered sugar
4 tablespoons room temperature butter
2 tablespoons all-purpose flour
1 room temperature egg
1 teaspoon vanilla

Directions:
1. Grease a cake mold with butter. The mold should fit inside the cooker and be oven-safe, but not glass.
2. Put a trivet in the pressure cooker.
3. Add 2 cups of water.
4. In a separate container, whisk the flour and sugar together.
5. In another bowl, melt the chocolate chips and butter until smooth.

6. Add the egg and vanilla into the chocolate mixture, and blend.
7. Pour in the flour/sugar into the chocolate and blend again.
8. Fill your cake mold half full.
9. Place the mold on top of the trivet in the pressure cooker.
10. Secure the lid and cook on high for 8 minutes.
11. Turn off the cooker and let the pressure come down by itself.

Cooking Tip
To tell if the cake is ready, you can't really do the toothpick trick because the middle is supposed to be gooey. If the cakes look puffy and cooked, they're probably good. You don't want to overcook lava cakes.

12. Invert on a plate and serve!

Nutritional information (per serving):
Calories - 360
Protein- 5
Carbs - 40
Fat - 23
Fiber - 3

French Lemon Creme Pots
Serves: 6
Time: 1 hour, 30 minutes (20 minute cook time)

If you aren't a chocolate person or want something a little lighter and fresher after a heavy meal, these French lemon custards are the perfect idea. They are made from a few high-quality ingredients like fresh cream, milk, egg yolk, and lemon, and garnished with blackberries.

Ingredients:
6 egg yolks
1 cup fresh cream
1 cup whole milk
1 lemon
⅔cup white sugar
½ cup fresh blackberries

Directions:
1. Using a potato peeler, peel the lemon skin so you get wide strips.
2. In a saucepan, add the milk, cream, and zest strips on medium-high heat.
3. Stir until it begins to bubble.
4. Turn off the heat and let it cool for about a half hour.
5. When ready, pour the minimum amount of water required for your pressure cooker into the pressure cooker.
6. In a separate bowl, whisk the sugar with the egg yolks until the sugar dissolves.
7. Pour the cream/milk mixture slowly into the yolks.
8. Stir with your whisk to mix, but do not whip.
9. Pour this slowly through a strainer into a container with a spout, before pouring into your ramekins.
10. Cover in foil and place in the steamer basket in the pressure cooker. You may need to do a second batch.
11. Secure the pressure cooker lid and cook on high pressure for 10 minutes.

12. Turn off the cooker and let the pressure decrease naturally.
13. Remove the custards and check for doneness - they should be nearly solid.
14. Cool on the counter, uncovered, for 30-45 minutes.
15. Cover with plastic wrap and store in the fridge for further cooling.
16. Serve with fresh blackberries and a spoon!

Nutritional information (per serving):
Calories - 380
Protein- 8
Carbs - 46
Fat - 20
Fiber - 2

Eggless Vanilla Rava Cake

Serves: 4
Time: 50 minutes (17 minute cook time)

Rava is an Indian wheat product, and because of the yogurt also included in this recipe, you are assured a moist, delicious cake. The cake gets its sweetness from a little vanilla and sugar, but also some more interesting flavors from cardamom powder and saffron. It's a great option if you're dairy-free and/or want a cake that isn't too sweet.

Ingredients:
¾ cup rava
¾ cup yogurt
½ cup sugar (can go up to ¾ cup)
3 tablespoons (+ ½ teaspoon) melted butter
4-5 strands crushed saffron
2-3 pinches cardamom powder

¾ teaspoon vanilla
¾ teaspoon baking powder
¼ teaspoon baking soda

Directions:
1. Mix the sugar, yogurt, and rava together.
2. Keep this mixture covered for 30 minutes before continuing.
3. Next, add the baking soda, baking powder, butter, saffron, cardamom, and vanilla.
4. Preheat your pressure cooker without water.
5. Grease a cake pan (that fits in the cooker) with butter.
6. Fill with the minimum required amount of water, for safety.
7. Pour in the batter and place the pan (uncovered) on the trivet carefully inside the cooker.
8. Secure the pressure cooker and cook on high pressure for 15 minutes.
9. Quick-release the pressure.
10. Check the cake with a toothpick. It probably won't be done, but you need to keep cooking it for about 10 more minutes on a low setting like "browning," where you don't need the pressure cooker lid secured.
11. When the cake's edges are golden brown and the center of the cake is done, it's ready.
12. Turn off the cooker and cover the cooker for 5 more minutes so the cake can set.
13. Invert the cake onto a plate.
14. Toppings include frosting, nuts, fruit, shaved coconut, and so on.

Nutritional information (per serving):
Calories - 225
Protein- 4

Carbs - 30
Fat - 10
Fiber - 0

Mascarpone-Stuffed Red Wine Pears

Serves: 6
Time: 7 hours minimum (25 minute cook time)

Fresh pears are poached in red wine and then filled with impossibly creamy, sweetened Mascarpone. This is truly an adult dessert and will make you feel like you're a gourmet chef. There's a bit more prep to this dish than other recipes, but it's mostly waiting, and not actual work.

Ingredients:
6 peeled Bartlett pears
1 bottle of red wine
1-2 cups water
1-2 cups white sugar
2 bay leaves
2 cloves
2 cinnamon sticks
1 fresh vanilla bean
16-ounces Mascarpone cheese
½ cup powdered sugar
½ cup whipped cream
2 teaspoons ground cinnamon

Directions:
1. Pour one bottle of red wine into the pressure cooker along with all the spices in the first list of ingredients. Scrape out the vanilla bean seeds before throwing in the whole stem.
2. Pour in 1 cup of water and stir well.

3. Put your pears in the cooker and make sure they are completely submerged.
4. Secure the lid and set the electric cooker time for 20 minutes.
5. Prepare the filling by mixing everything in the second list together.
6. Put the mixture into a piping bag and refrigerate.
7. When the pears are done, quick-release the pressure.
8. Turn off the cooker and let everything cool.
9. Put the whole pressure cooker in the fridge overnight or at least 6 hours.
10. When time is up, take out the pot.
11. Carefully remove the pears.
12. Pick out the bay leaves, cloves, and vanilla stem.
13. Pour out 3 cups of the wine from the cooker and save. Get rid of the rest.
14. Pour the 3 cups back into the cooker, add 2 tablespoons butter, and turn the cooker on the lowest heat setting to thicken.
15. Bring to a boil and reduce until it looks like syrup.
16. Carefully remove the cores from the pears and plate.
17. Get out the piping tool from yesterday and pipe the Mascarpone into the center of each pear.
18. Ladle the wine syrup over the pears and serve!

Nutritional information (1 pear per serving):
Calories - 338
Protein- 2
Carbs - 42
Fat - 14
Fiber - 6

Chocolate Bread Pudding
Serves: 6

Time: 30 minutes (15 minute cook time)

Bread pudding is a comfort-food dessert. It's warm, sweet, and often studded with raisins. This version swaps out raisins for dark chocolate, making things a bit more intense and rich. If you're looking to switch up your baking routine, this is an easy and rewarding recipe to try.

Ingredients:
2 cups water
1 cup whole milk
2 big eggs
5 tablespoons white sugar
7 ounces of stale Brioche bread, ¾ of an inch cubes with crusts cut off
3.5 ounces of bittersweet chocolate, cut into chips
1 tablespoon chopped butter
1 tablespoon raw sugar
1 teaspoon vanilla
A pinch of salt

Directions:
1. Pour two cups of water into the pressure cooker and set down the trivet inside.
2. Grease a dish with butter.
3. In a bowl, whisk the sugar and eggs together.
4. Add the salt, vanilla, and milk.
5. Mix the bread cubes in the dish with your hands and rest for 5 minutes.
6. Mix for a second time before pouring everything into the dish. You can squish down the bread to make it fit.
7. Add the chocolate and mix around a bit.
8. Wait 5 minutes and then mix for a last time.
9. Put the dish (uncovered) into the cooker.

10. Secure the lid and cook for 10-15 minutes on high pressure.
11. When time is up, turn off the cooker and wait until the pressure decreases naturally.
12. After 10 minutes, release any leftover pressure.
13. Take out the dish and sprinkle with the raw sugar and the little chopped bits of butter.
14. Broil for 5 minutes.
15. Serve with vanilla ice cream and enjoy!

Nutritional information (per serving):
Calories - 289
Protein- 7
Carbs - 45
Fat - 10
Fiber - 1

Cinnamon-Stewed Fruits

Serves: 6
Time: 10 minutes (5 minute cook time)

This simple dish is deceptively easy and can be thrown together with just some dried fruit, wine, sugar, and cinnamon. It's great for cooler nights when you want something warm and cozy, but not super heavy or rich.

Ingredients:
1 pound mixed dried fruit
1 cup water
1 cup red wine
¾ cup packed brown sugar
2 slices of lemon
1 cinnamon stick

Directions:

1. Mix the wine, sugar, water, lemon, and cinnamon stick together in the pressure cooker.
2. Bring to a boil on the "sauté" setting and simmer until the sugar is dissolved.
3. Throw in the fruit.
4. Secure the pressure cooker lid and cook on high for 5 minutes.
5. You can eat as is, with whipped cream, or on top of vanilla ice cream.

Nutritional information (per serving):

Calories - 379

Protein- 2

Carbs - 88

Fat - 0

Fiber - 5.8

Maple Syrup Apple Flan w/ Cinnamon

Serves: 6

Time: 18 minutes (8 minute cook time)

Flan is a creamy, custard caramel top that is very sweet. This version adds more texture and a little bit of spice with apples and cinnamon. You can also use pears or peaches if you want if apples aren't in season.

Ingredients:

2 ½ cups milk

6 tablespoons sugar

5 tablespoons maple syrup

3 whole eggs

3 egg yolks

2 peeled and cut apples (¼ inch)

¼ teaspoon cinnamon
¼ teaspoon vanilla

Directions:
1. Combine the cinnamon and maple syrup in a saucepan over the stove.
2. Add in the apple slices and simmer until the fruit is tender.
3. Divide up this mixture into 6 greased ramekins.
4. In a separate bowl, whisk the egg yolks and eggs together.
5. Add in the sugar, milk, and vanilla.
6. Pour carefully into the ramekins and cover with foil.
7. Prepare the pressure cooker with the water.
8. Lower the ramekins into the steamer basket. You may have to do two batches.
9. Secure the lid and cook on high pressure for 8 minutes.
10. When the timer sounds, turn off the cooker and let the pressure decrease on its own.
11. After the pressure is gone, wait another 10 minutes with the lid closed.
12. Take out the custards and let them cool before storing in the fridge.
13. You can serve from the ramekins or use a knife to remove the flans.

Nutritional information (per serving):
Calories - 241
Protein- 8
Carbs - 37
Fat - 8
Fiber – 0

Epilogue

I hope you enjoyed reading this book and are excited to start making some (or all) of these 100 electric pressure cooker recipes! I tried to include as much variety as possible, including vegetarian and vegan options. Electric pressure cookers are one of the greatest kitchen tools you could have, especially if you are short on time, but love making good food. Electric pressure cookers allow you to experiment and be adventurous, but without all the work and long cooking times that other cooking methods require.

I've also included two indexes from my other book on pressure cooking, because they are useful and still apply to electric pressure cookers specifically. You can look up general main ingredients (beef brisket, chicken breasts, brown rice, etc.) and see how long they are supposed to cook in both a stove top or electric pressure cooker, and on what pressure. The second index lets you know how to convert slow cooker to pressure cookers in general, so combined with the how-to in chapter 6, you can easily convert slow cooker recipes to electric pressure cookers.

Again, thank you for reading this book, and happy cooking!

Index 1- Time Conversion Charts

Food	Electric Pressure Cooker (10-12 psi) Time	Stove top Pressure Cooker (13-15 psi) Time	Pressure Selection
Beef (brisket)	70	50	High
Beef (ground)	6	6	High
Beef (ribs)	60	45	High
Chicken breast (boneless)	1	1	High
Chicken (ground)	5	4	High
Chicken (whole)	20	15	High
Eggs (poached)	2	2	Low
Lamb chops	7	3	High
Pork chops	8	6	High
Pork ribs	20	15	High
Pork sausage	10	8	High
Roast beef (medium)	8 to 10	8	High
Turkey breast (sliced)	7 to 9	7	High
Turkey leg	35	30	High
Fish fillet	3	2	Low
Salmon	6	5	Low
Shrimp	2	1	Low
Trout	12	8	Low
Oats (steel-cut)	3	3	High
Quinoa	1	1	High
Brown rice	20	18	High
Jasmine rice (rinsed)	1	1	Low or high
White (long-grain) rice	3	3	Low or high

Artichoke hearts	3	3	Low or high
Broccoli	3 to 5	3 to 5	Low or high
Carrots (sliced)	1 to 2	1 to 2	Low or high
Cauliflower (florets)	2 to 3	2 to 3	Low or high
Corn on the cob	5	5	Low or high
Onions	3	3	Low or high
Peas (fresh or frozen)	2 to 3	2 to 3	Low or high
Bell peppers	3 to 4	3 to 4	Low or high
Whole sweet potatoes	15	10	High
Butternut squash (halves)	6	6	Low or high
Apples	3	2	High
Black beans (soaked)	6	4	High
White beans (soaked)	8	6	High

Index 2 - Converting Slow Cooker Recipes to a Pressure Cooker

Since lots of people don't have a pressure cooker, most of their favorite recipes are usually made in the oven, on a burner, or in a slow cooker. When you start using a pressure cooker, you'll want to know how to convert recipes. There are lots of websites that include "Recipe Calculators," where you list the ingredients in the original recipe and the website lets you know how to cook everything in the pressure cooker. When you buy a pressure cooker, the owner's manual also usually includes a section on how to translate slow cooker recipes. However, for your convenience, let's take a look at the basics when it comes to converting any recipe to a pressure cooker. Here are the four most important questions you should be asking:

- How much cooking time does the original recipe call for?
- How much liquid does the final product include?
- Which veggies are "aromatic" and should therefore be cooked first?
- Will all the food fit into the pressure cooker or do I need to do two batches?

Pressure cooking is much faster than other methods. Find out the cook time for the original recipe (not the total prep time) and reduce it by ⅔. That's how long you will cook the meal in the pressure cooker.

The next step is to look at the liquid. Determine how much liquid the recipe ends up with, not how much you actually add. This is because other cooking methods result in a lot of evaporated liquid, while pressure cooking keeps most of the liquid. Write down how much liquid you want in the end product, plus an additional ½ cup. This will be used before you add the other ingredients, because the pressure cooker needs it to generate pressure.

Look at the vegetables in the recipe and determine which are "aromatic." These include celery, onions, garlic, carrots, and peppers. In a pressure cooker, you should always sauté these veggies first with a coat of oil on the bottom, so you can create a lovely flavor base for the rest of your ingredients.

If necessary, divide up the original recipe in half. Pressure cookers may hold less food than the usual container you use. For safety, a pressure cooker should only be filled ⅔ of the way at a time. If your meal is bigger than this, you'll need to make it in two batches.

Once you have answered these four questions, follow the recipe as it is written in terms of what order to put in ingredients and how much spice to use. If you are still uncertain about a recipe, try to find a similar one that is specifically for a pressure cooker. You can compare what you came up with to the other recipe's instructions and make any adjustments if necessary.

From "Pressure Cooker – 100 Quick, Easy, and Healthy Pressure Cooker Recipes for Nourishing and Delicious Meals"

I hope the book was able to teach you how pressure cooking can simplify your everyday life.

If you enjoyed this book, then I'd like to ask you for a favor, would you be kind enough to leave a review for this book on Amazon? It'd be greatly appreciated!

Also, I would love to give you a bonus. Please email me at vanessa.olsen400p@gmail.com to avail the FREE Paleo Diet book.

Please check out my other books in Amazon:
- **Ketogenic Diet** - Achieve Rapid Weight Loss while Gaining Incredible Health and Energy
- **Ketogenic Diet Cookbook** - 80 Easy, Delicious, and Healthy Recipes to Help You Lose Weight, Boost Your Energy, and Prevent Cancer, Stroke and Alzheimer's
- **Ketogenic Diet-2 in 1 Box Set** - A Complete Guide to the Ketogenic Diet-115 Amazing Recipes for Weight Loss and Improved Health

- **Mediterranean Diet for Beginners** - 50 Amazing Recipes for Weight Loss and Improved Health
- **Mediterranean Diet Cookbook** - 105 Easy, Irresistible, and Healthy Recipes for Weight Loss and Improved Quality of Life While Minimizing the Risk of Disease
- **Mediterranean Diet-2 in 1 Box Set** - A Comprehensive Guide to the Mediterranean Diet-155 Mouth-Watering and Healthy Recipes to Help You Lose Weight, Increase Your Energy Level and Prevent Disease
- **Pressure Cooker Cookbook** - 100 Quick, Easy, and Healthy Pressure Cooker Recipes for Nourishing and Delicious Meals

Thank you and good luck!